C000273548

'You hold in your hand a very important b‹ about youth ministry has surfaced, ques Looking at denominational reports and s‹ begun wondering if youth ministry has f; exciting and important response. In *Faith Generation*, Shepherd shows that youth ministry does indeed have an important element to play in faith formation and one that can be deeply transformational. This book will inspire, stretch and enlighten any pastor, youth worker or parent who gives it the time it deserves.'

Andrew Root, Olson Baalson Associate Professor of Youth and Family Ministry, Luther Seminary, USA, and author of Bonhoeffer as Youth Worker

'This book should be essential reading for all concerned with the future of the Church. Drawing on his extensive experience as both a practitioner and researcher in youth ministry, Nick Shepherd highlights the challenge for the Church of faith transmission in a way which inspires and gives hope. Illuminated by direct quotations from many young people, the book offers a window into their faith and is enriched by the case studies of two very contrasting situations: suburban church and, urban outreach project. Nick offers a fresh approach to youth ministry that focuses on practices of identity, plausibility and reliability. This offers a new way to reframe work with children and young people and will be a valuable text for churches as well as those of us working in theological education with children, youth workers and clergy.'

The Revd Dr Sally Nash, Director, Midlands Institute for Children, Youth and Mission at St John's School of Mission, Nottingham, and Associate Minister at Hodge Hill Church, Birmingham

'*Faith Generation* is an important and timely contribution to the current debate around young people and the Church. This book makes it clear that most talk about youth ministry starts in the wrong place. It is a mistake to talk only about what the Church does or what youth leaders do. Youth ministry cannot just be about the next new programme for evangelism or discipleship or the next worship event that will renew the faith of young people. Nick Shepherd turns this way of thinking on its head and asks how young people are themselves active in making their own faith. This way of thinking is desperately needed because it puts young people at the centre of the way the Church thinks about ministry, mission and worship. By looking at young people as active participants in ministry, he develops ground-breaking new perspectives that everyone who cares about young people and the Church really needs to know about.'

Professor Pete Ward, Professorial Fellow in Ecclesiology and Ethnography, St John's College/Department of Theology and Religion, Durham University

'Everyone knows the Church faces a huge challenge to communicate the Christian faith to younger people. Nick Shepherd has a lifetime of experience in youth work and educating youth workers, and is uniquely placed to write *Faith Generation*. Thankfully, this isn't a book that just tells us a problem, it gives us helpful ways to begin to reverse the decline. A must-read for every church leader.'

Canon Mark Russell, Chief Executive, Church Army

'Nick Shepherd's *Faith Generation: Retaining Young People and Growing the Church* is essential reading for all who are interested in nurturing young Christians, bringing young people to faith, working in Christian youth work or who work in schools. It is also essential reading for anyone interested in growing the Church and the vital task of renewal and reform.

'With a masterly grasp of the history and theology of Christians working with young people, this book, emerging from a doctoral thesis, is never heavy. Close study of two young people's projects and careful listening to, and ample quotation from, young people bring a lightness of touch that makes this an easy read but one that stimulates a great deal of thought. Using the device of *choice*, *sense* and *use*, Shepherd examines the way in which young people make faith decisions, experience God and perceive faith as part of crafting their lives. Helpful questions at the end of each chapter make this an ideal text for a church school faith group, chaplains, governors or, even better, joint work between youth workers, clergy and church school staff and governors.

'From my own school leadership angle, this book has challenged me to think about the extent to which faith development in school is approached coherently with the nurture (or otherwise) young Christians, and young people generally, receive in their families and in the wider Church. To what extent is there "reasonable porousness" between these areas of a young person's life? *Faith Generation* raises the question of the extent to which we, in church schools, can offer young people "plausibility shelters" as they explore belief in a situation of church decline.'

Fr Richard Peers, Director of Education, Diocese of Liverpool

'*Faith Generation* is a hugely helpful overview of the latest research and thinking around youth ministry in the UK. In this bold book, Shepherd tackles head on the decline besetting the Church, and provides fascinating reflections on the possible historical, social and cultural causes. No longer can we rest on our laurels and hope in vain for a reversal of the decline; we must learn, as *Faith Generation* so robustly demonstrates, to cultivate faith with young people who have no prior experience of church at all. Shepherd places youth ministry high up on the agenda of the Church, and is a powerful advocate for the relationship between church growth and thriving youth work. *Faith Generation* is a rallying cry to the Church to remember once again the importance of youth ministry, and offers insightful solutions, backed by in-depth research, about how to put this into practice.'

Phoebe Thompson, Head of Research, Youthscape,
and a former editor of Youthwork Magazine

FAITH GENERATION

Retaining young people and growing the Church

Nick Shepherd

First published in Great Britain in 2016

Society for Promoting Christian Knowledge
36 Causton Street
London SW1P 4ST
www.spck.org.uk

The author and publisher have made every effort to ensure that the external website and
email addresses included in this book are correct and up to date at the time of
going to press. The author and publisher are not responsible for
the content, quality or continuing accessibility of the sites.

British Library Cataloguing-in-Publication Data
A catalogue record for this book is available from the British Library

ISBN 978–0–281–07388–7
eBook ISBN 978–0–281–07389–4

Typeset by Graphicraft Limited, Hong Kong
First printed in Great Britain by Ashford Colour Press
Subsequently digitally printed in Great Britain

eBook by Graphicraft Limited, Hong Kong

Produced on paper from sustainable forests

In memory of Tom Conway,
an example of faith for any generation

Contents

Illustrations

Figures

Table

Acknowledgements

It is the insights of young people that lie at the heart of this book. I would most of all, then, like to thank the young people who were participants in the research I conducted and the many others who have influenced my thinking. In preparing this book I am grateful to those who reviewed and helped me rewrite the manuscript, especially to Sally Nash and Tracey Messenger. Several of the concepts presented here were developed through the Lectures in Youth, Culture and Church I gave at the Princeton Seminary Youth Ministry Forum in 2013 and I am thankful to the organizers for the opportunity to bring my ideas to that event. Understanding comes through conversation, and without my wife Bridget and friends and colleagues most of my ideas would be less informed and remain unformed. On this project Andy Root, Ali Campbell, Simon Davies and Gretchen Schoon-Tanis have been highly influential in shaping my thinking. Finally, I am indebted to my mentor and friend Professor Pete Ward. Pete has pioneered the academic study of youth ministry, and without his vision and generous enthusiasm many of us would still be scratching our heads wondering what on earth we are trying to do.

Introduction
The urgent need for faith generation

It was just before the start of a youth group session I was helping to lead that the profound comment came. I was chatting with one of the girls in the group about the ups and downs of her week at school. I can't now recall the exact events, but it had been one of those weeks where she had felt her faith was under pressure. There had been arguments in a religious education (RE) class about religion being a problem in the world – a point that the teacher had asked her to defend. There was a friend confiding in her about a situation that was tough to handle because, as the friend acknowledged, since she was a Christian she knew she would listen to her! Then just before coming to the group there had been a fall-out with parents about a night out that had gone on later than expected. Then came the phrase that struck me and has stuck with me ever since: 'You know, Nick, I am *trying to be a Christian.*'

I had been involved in youth ministry at this point for about ten years and knew full well that young people needed to be active in owning and forming their own faith, but there was something that caught my imagination in this moment. Two things fell into place in my understanding of the role and purpose of youth ministry, which began the journey to this book. The first was that I probably did not appreciate fully the experience and task of 'trying to be Christian' that this young woman and her contemporaries have – the complexities and challenge of holding and expressing faith in an environment that was either hostile or indifferent; the ways in which being a Christian also, though, drew her into being someone who could be relied on; the ways in which the dimensions of all this activity of being Christian are hidden or hard to express when conflicts over commitment or behaviour

1

come to the fore. The second thought followed obviously from this. Does youth ministry actually help young people trying to be Christian – and if so, how?

This book presents an account of the experiences of young people trying to be Christian and a model of youth ministry built upon understanding faith in this generation. Such an approach is vital if we are to address the pressing need of helping children and young people form faith, faith that will be sustained and sustain them in the world in which they live. In many parts of the world, including the UK, we have a decline in faith generation. Christian faith is falling and failing for young people.

The need to address this issue is one of the headline conclusions from the Church of England's recent study into church growth. The *From Anecdote to Evidence* report in 2014 concluded that if we want our churches to be healthy and growing places, we could do much worse than begin with a focused attention on our work with children and young people. If we are serious about investing in 'focal ministries' that support the life of communities of faith, this research also suggests that the most fruitful investment we can make is to employ, or at the very least deploy, someone to coordinate this task.

> There is an urgent need to focus on children, young people and their parents and a challenge to identify how the church can best invest in people, programmes and strategies which will encourage young people actively to continue exploring faith.[1]

These insights in growth and children and youth ministry came from the Church Growth Research Programme,[2] summarized in *From Anecdote to Evidence*. This work found that almost half of Anglican churches had fewer than five young people under 16. Churches with no young people at all are also more likely to be in decline. Conversely, churches with young people are twice as likely to be growing churches, and where they employ a children

---

[1] *From Anecdote to Evidence: Findings from the Church Growth Research Programme 2011–13* (London: The Church of England, 2014), 24.

[2] <www.churchgrowthresearch.org.uk>.

or youth worker they are half as likely as other churches to be in decline. In comparison with other appointments a church can make, this suggests that employing someone in this role is the most effective lay appointment a church can make in terms of growth. While the data drawn on for the report can only show an *association* between growth and children and youth work, it does provide significant evidence to back up the call for prioritizing this area of church life.

This is an argument that many involved in Christian youth work and ministries have been pressing for some time and it is good to finally have some evidence to back up the anecdotal accounts of the importance of this area of mission and ministry. Like all good researchers the authors of *From Anecdote to Evidence* take great care not to overstate the implication that if a church does focus on youth and children's work, growth will naturally follow. They are also cautious about stating that this focus is the cause of growth, as opposed to a sign of growth being managed well. I understand this caution, but wish to argue here that not only is there a link between children and youth ministry and growth, there is a relationship. We see health and growth in a church because attention to ministry and mission with children and young people (if done well) causes this.

To support my case I will draw on research of my own, under-taken over a number of years with young people and their youth leaders, into what difference youth ministry might make for young people 'trying to be Christians'. In conducting this I spent three years talking with young people about their experiences of being Christian and observing and discussing with them the youth min-istry projects in which they participated. This close-up research on actual practice offers evidence of its own into what works in youth ministry. By looking at the detail of the activities that this ministry involves, and by asking young people how this relates to their experience of being Christian, we move closer to identifying the causes of growth connected with youth ministry suggested by the *From Anecdote to Evidence* research. Looking at this detail gives a greater insight into why this ministry makes a difference, shows what it does for the young people who participate in this provision and highlights its important role in shaping healthy church life. As we move through the examples of the youth ministry projects I researched, there will also be benefit in thinking about the actual practice you might be engaged in, or be able to observe. Some insights may resonate and others may not. The critical issue is to try to discern not only what we can do, but also why this is important. If we can identify clear principles, these then help to inform practice in a variety of contexts. This is the aim of this book – to identify what the challenges are for faith generation and to outline a model of youth ministry to address these.

It is clear both from *From Anecdote to Evidence*, and from wider work at the moment, that in speaking of work with children and young people we cannot focus only on the older age group, namely, teenagers. Since it was this group that was the focus of my research it is the area that I can strongly evidence here. However, from what the young people themselves say, backed up by writing focused on the importance of children and family ministry, many of my conclusions have broader applicability. I will, though, be focusing on work with young people, which I argue has a particular importance in considering faith formation.

By the end of the book I hope to have made a case that the urgent action on work with children, young people and their parents called for in *From Anecdote to Evidence* is necessary and achievable. My main point will be that we need to take action because faith formation in our contemporary context doesn't just 'happen' – it needs to be stimulated and supported. This is the main thrust of describing this activity as *faith generation*. This approach is perhaps obvious in the context of mission – in the ways in which we might seek to engage and encourage young people outside the Church to enquire and explore about what being Christians might mean. My contention is that this is equally true for young people who have been 'brought up to believe'. This means looking more closely at what it is actually like for these young people in the journey towards young adulthood and asking the question, 'What do we need to do as communities of faith to help provide the conditions and catalyst for faith generation?' From this we can begin to piece together some strategies that might help foster faith generation. I will also argue that when we do this, it not only has an impact on young people themselves but also acts as a stimulus for growth within church communities and for the local church within its community. This then is a 'why-how-to' book – we first need to understand *why* we need to focus our action in this area and what impact we are looking for, before we proceed to consider *how to* do this.

I will begin by looking in closer detail at the trends and influences that lie behind the findings presented in *From Anecdote to Evidence*. While it is encouraging to know that there are signs of growth, it is important to read these against the context of decline, particularly that of young people's participation in church. This decline has been continual for some time and this then is our first 'why' question. Why is this decline happening and what are the reasons for this?

Central will be the idea that the eventuality of future generations forming and expressing a vibrant Christian faith is no longer a 'natural process'. It does not happen automatically, even where parents and others are supportive and active in wanting to raise their children in the faith they hold. The passing on of faith from one generation to the next has always required an active engage-ment in telling the story and helping young people grow into their own understanding, yet in our situation of decline this is increas-ingly problematic – the Church is experiencing a 'general failure in passing on faith from one generation to the next'.[3] Understanding this helps to identify what is different in the places where we see growth and the links this has to the focused youth work and ministry happening in these contexts. From this understanding we will have greater insight into what can be gained from investing in and enhancing our work among children and young people.

Before looking at the impact that youth work and ministry has for young people 'trying to be Christian', it is important to identify what I mean by this activity. What are we talking about

---

[3] A. Crockett and D. Voas, 'Generations of Decline: Religious Change in 20th-Century Britain', *Journal for the Scientific Study of Religion* 45, no. 4 (2006), 567–84; David Voas and Alasdair Crockett, 'Religion in Britain: Neither Believing nor Belonging', *Sociology* 39, no. 1 (2005), 11–28.

when we encourage churches to engage in this activity as a focused ministry? What does it look like and whom does it involve? This overview is mainly to help situate the insights and experiences of the young people I talked to and is not meant to be a comprehensive review of youth work and ministry. Such an overview would undoubtedly be helpful as we seek to invest in growing this area of activity, but it is not provided here! Important parameters, though, do need to be set around the basis of this work – youth ministry – as providing *distinct learning, intentional relationships* and *formative practices* for young people trying to be Christian. These are not the only ways to define this activity, but are the ones that I think are most pertinent to the issue of faith generation, which is my focus here.[4]

The two opening chapters set the scene for exploring faith generation, for looking at why youth ministry is an important activity in supporting young people in forming and expressing faith. In Chapters 3, 4 and 5 I explore how young people's participation in youth ministry helps enable them to form and express faith. Essentially I argue that for young people there are three key challenges to faith formation that they must identify and address. These challenges are *making the implausible choice, making coherent sense* and *making reliable use* of faith. These phrases capture the crucial dimensions of forming faith in our contemporary context as young people experience this task.

To act towards faith generation, youth ministry needs to bolster and boost this activity. The requirement of choosing to believe, and the continuing implications of this for young people, is a powerful social pressure on their identity, whether a young person has been brought up to believe or has been brought into belief later in life. The capacity of youth ministry to help in this choice, and to facilitate ongoing choice, is the first factor in addressing decline. Youth ministry must play a role in helping to make faith plausible in the modern world and helping young people to establish their own Christian presence.

---

[4] See Sally Nash and Jo Whitehead, eds, *Christian Youth Work in Theory and Practice: A Handbook* (London: SCM Press, 2014).

Young people too need to make sense of God in their own way in their own world. This may be obvious to those of us who feel we have a handle on it, but on reflection it perhaps shouldn't be. When young people talk about their experience of God – in fact their need for an experience of God – they tell us all something crucial about the pressure of holding faith in what can be termed a secular age. When young people tell us of the struggles they have in making sense of this God in the face of the cynicism of others and the scepticism created by the trials of life, they express this as a challenge to their sense of identity. Youth ministry plays a valuable part in setting the space for making sense of faith as an issue of identity as well as understanding. Done well, this can also help communities of faith share in this task and take direction from insights.

As young people begin to demonstrate to themselves that the life of faith is useful, and that their lives might be useful to God in his world, we see the importance of focusing intentionally on faith generation. As adults we may feel that teenage faith in God is a little too self-focused. Yet this is what might well be needed for many young people – someone to give something extra to their sense of self. We may feel that the shape of young people's spirituality is often a little self-indulgent. However, surely our faith does have to be useful to us. Being Christian ought to help lead us towards an abundant life, a meaningful life and a sense of a fulfilled life. If we start by listening to how being Christian helps young people negotiate their immediate needs in seeking this fullness of life, we can then seek to engage in deeper conversations about what a deeper life of discipleship might look like. Conversely, we may find that such a life is already richly present, but we are not accustomed to recognizing it because it looks different from the discipleship of adult believers. The activities of youth ministry can provide a challenging environment for young people to nudge forward a wider sense of engagement in life, as disciples, to test and deepen the reliability of their faith.

These activities are all crucial for the task of faith generation in the context in which we live, and they form the basis of the model of faith generation I outline in Chapter 6. Faith generation requires action to address the plausibility, identity and reliability of faith in a secular age. Engaging in youth ministry shaped by these principles and practices is the way in which we can take urgent action to stem and reverse decline. This in itself is sufficient argument for a greater focus on this activity within our churches. Yet the effect of this faith generation is not limited to young people alone. Focused work on faith generation among children and young people has a direct impact on the church communities of which they are a part and on the communities where we are seeking to make connections. This impact underscores why this work should be prioritized if we wish to see growth in the context of decline. This, as I will conclude in Chapter 7, can be achieved in any church context, whether it has a small base to start from or a more extensive approach to youth ministry already.

1

Decline, growth and signposts for change

---

*In Britain institutional religion now has a half-life of one
generation, to borrow the terminology of radioactive decay.
The generation now in middle age has produced children
who are only half as likely as they are to attend church, to
identify themselves as belonging to a denomination, or to say
that belief is important to them.* (*David Voas*[1])

In 2014 the Church of England produced a significant report outlining three years' worth of research into church growth entitled
From Anecdote to Evidence. The aim of the report was to provide
a clearer understanding of where growth might be occurring, and
the factors that support this. While specific to Anglican expressions
and initiatives, given an observable trend in other research that
indicates decline is now punctuated with signs of growth,[2] this
evidence is helpful in determining the focus for continued action
and reflection on the health and growth of the Church in England.

The report presents a buoyant picture where growth is observable in 18 per cent of churches and over half are also now seen
as relatively stable. A dose of realism is apparent in that 27 per
cent of churches are in decline and there are some general trends
that should still give cause for concern. Case studies in the research
show that growth is not confined to a particular tradition but

---

[1] David Voas, 'Children and Youth Ministry and Church Growth', *Praxeis* 1, no. 1 (2014):
3–8 (3).

[2] Peter Brierley, *The Tide Is Running Out* (London: Christian Research, 2001); Peter Brierley,
*Pulling Out of the Nosedive: A Contemporary Picture of Churchgoing: What the 2005 English
Church Census Reveals* (London: Christian Research, 2006).

includes parish churches, Fresh Expressions and church plants, and cathedrals (largely because these are the priorities for the Church Commissioners who funded the research).[3] The report first seeks to show where signs of growth are apparent and what factors might be present to cause or stimulate this. Among these, clear leadership, collaborative ministry (between lay and ordained), being a welcoming community and actively connecting with the wider community are given attention. It is not surprising, then, that these factors have received particular attention in strategic documents and books on church leadership.[4] What *is* perhaps surprising, and a little disappointing, is a general lack of response to one particular key finding from this research, namely that there is a clear association between children and youth ministry and growth.[5]

Actively engaging children and teenagers is highlighted as an associated trait in three quarters of growing churches.[6] Churches that employ a youth worker are only half as likely to be in decline as those that do not have this resource. From the perspective of growth, employing a children or youth worker is the most effective lay appointment a church can make. Beyond this, the association between growth and children and youth work shows that worship services designed for children, a youth programme, camps and retreats for young people and connections to a church school are the elements of this ministry that are strongly associated with growth.[7]

What is harder to identify is why this is the case. Why are these activities vital and why do they bring vitality? This question of

---

[3] *From Anecdote to Evidence: Findings from the Church Growth Research Programme 2011–13* (London: The Church of England, 2014), 17–19.

[4] Bob Jackson, *What Makes Churches Grow? Vision and Practice in Effective Mission* (London: Church House Publishing, 2015).

[5] I will use the term 'children and youth ministry' and occasionally 'youth ministry' to refer to a broad range of activities that are connected by the central theme of being provided for, or put on to serve, the ministry needs of school-aged children at both primary and secondary levels. This includes what some see as family ministry. My main area of expertise in this field is work with older young people and it is on this experience that I will largely draw. I will, however, where possible, identify where narrower distinctions are required.

[6] *From Anecdote to Evidence*, 12.

[7] *From Anecdote to Evidence*, 26. The association with a church school is perhaps an obvious factor. This is explored in some depth within the background research document – one or more factors are required: <www.churchgrowthresearch.org.uk>.

'causation' is not an issue that the researchers feel able to comment upon in this report. There is a difficulty in establishing the distinction between correspondence and causality – do churches grow because they have youth ministry or do growing churches have youth ministry because they are growing? A reason for arguing that intentionally focusing on children and youth ministry is a factor that promotes growth is found, though, in placing this evidence in the context of the more general problem of decline that recent 'growth' strategies have sought to address, namely that our key problem is a decline in young people remaining in church.

Our problem with decline still lies in our lack of ability to pass on the faith to the next generation, a problem at a crucial tipping point given that nearly half of churches have fewer than five under-16-year-olds connected to them. Churches that are growing may simply require identifiable family and/or youth ministry activities to manage the increased numbers of young people they have; families might move to churches with such activities and concentrate the numbers we have in such churches. Yet this association with growth, and growth by association, in my view does not fully take into account what is actually happening in youth ministry. An assumption that effective youth ministry is a sign of growth caused by other factors runs the risk of overlooking how this area of practice is crucial in addressing the issues that children and young people themselves identify as challenges to their own belief and engagement in church. If decline in young people's continuing participation in church life remains our primary problem and at the same time youth ministry is strongly associated with growth, is it not fair to assume some causal link between these two key findings?

There are some very basic principles behind putting children and youth ministry activities in place that might help promote growth. These are not what I intend to explore here, though they are in my view strong arguments alone for putting such priorities in place. The first is that by focusing on children's and young people's activities churches enhance their community connections – and also specifically connect to families who are moving to certain areas, moving through key life-stages and in some circumstances looking for ways to reconnect with the faith that might have been a part of their childhood. This 'social contact' basis for growth is apparent, especially in the ways in which Messy Church, for instance, has re-engaged some families that had become disconnected from churches in their areas.[8] It is my view, however, that effective children and youth ministry actually lies at the heart of these growing churches for a reason – it is a key requirement for growth. This is not to say, however, that all churches that have such ministries are growing or will grow. What is important to note is that in the midst of decline – and in particular generational decline – these are places where the transmission of faith between generations is intentionally or consequently being addressed. Further, since the general picture is one of decline, what might we learn from such examples that might be more deliberately put in place elsewhere?

If you grew up in a church, or came to faith through church youth work, no doubt you will recognize these activities immediately. You may even have a sense of the personal importance this participation had for you. As someone who has spent the past 20 years arguing for urgent investment in children and youth work, I find it comforting to have this level of institutional affirmation of the association youth ministry can have with growth. However, without tackling the question of why this is important we cannot really begin to address the questions of 'what' and 'how'.

This perspective may not strike you as surprising, given that I am someone who has spent his working life implementing, and latterly arguing for, an urgent focus on youth ministry and mission. This does not mean, however, that we should be uncritical of what is undertaken and what we have achieved. While association with signs of growth is encouraging, it is also true that much of what we have done in youth ministry over the past 20 years may be considered to be highly ineffective!

Within youth ministry this has provoked reflection on whether the focus of practice has been adequate. Some have argued that a greater attention to working with families is preferable to the peer-focused youth ministry that we have broadly adopted across

---

[8] Highlighted in *Church Growth Research Project Report on Strand 3b: An Analysis of Fresh Expressions of Church and Church Plants Begun in the Period 1992–2012* (Sheffield: Church Army Research Unit, 2013).

most denominations.[9] The role that parents play, or don't play, in the formation of their children's faith has also been given attention – in suggesting both that the weakness in passing on faith lies here and that this is where we are best drawn to put resources.[10] There is also increased emphasis now on children's ministry – on understanding the ways in which faith is nurtured and helping parents engage more effectively in supporting their children's faith formation.[11] Beyond these ministry-focused reflections there is also a concern for how we might reconnect and re-engage with the young people who have had no contact with the Church for generations – who belong to families with little connection to church or live in areas where churches have little connection to their communities. The declining number of young people in church needs to be set against a backdrop in which the majority of young people in the UK, Europe and increasingly the USA don't go to church![12]

These remain important questions and they are part of the bigger picture I want to address in this chapter. What's the problem? Why are young people leaving the Church and why is the Church no longer a part of the landscape of young people's sense of spirituality and religion? These are the questions that lie at the heart of whether the strategy of employing a person to lead and develop specific programmes to nurture children and young people's faith, providing communal support and resources for parents and beyond this engaging with young people outside the Church, is likely to lead to growth. Or, to put it another way, whether growth is possible at all if we *don't* focus on these tasks.

---

[9] Mark DeVries, *Family-Based Youth Ministry: Reaching the Been-There, Done-That Generation* (Downer's Grove, IL: IVP, 1994).

[10] *From Anecdote to Evidence* highlights the fact that there is a problem in parents' views of their active role in faith formation (25). See also Kenda Creasy Dean, *Almost Christian: What the Faith of Our Teenagers Is Telling the American Church* (New York: Oxford University Press, 2010).

[11] Ivy Beckwith, *Postmodern Children's Ministry: Ministry to Children in the 21st Century* (El Cajon, CA: Youth Specialties, 2004).

[12] For a summary of this phenomenon in a number of religions and contexts, see Naomi Schaefer Riley, *Got Religion? How Churches, Mosques, and Synagogues Can Bring Young People Back* (West Conshohocken, PA: Templeton Press, 2014).

Faith in decline: accepting the evidence on generational decline

The signs of growth highlighted in *From Anecdote to Evidence* are encouraging, and the call for urgent action to foster these is welcome. Yet, within this, it would be a mistake to miss the point that the backdrop to these findings remains the reality of decline. Alongside natural decline as members of older generations die, the particular problem we still have is that young people are leaving the Church and that mission work among young people has a negligible impact on this. The first priority we have is to accept this decline as the 'brutal reality' we face, to try to understand why it is happening and to do something about it.

A steady stream of research indicates that this trend has been with us since before the 1950s and that it is deep and continuing. In the 1990s, data provided a new impetus that 'reaching and keeping' teenagers should be a priority for the Church; analysis of the English Church Attendance Survey revealed that on average churches were 'losing' 140,000 young people aged 14–16 every week.[13] This trend was later extended to include 'tweenagers' who, by the age of 11, were already seen to dissociate from the Church as soon as other options for leisure activities become viable in their family lives.[14] At the turn of the new millennium, the threat was that the Church might be 'one generation from extinction' – with dissociation or disaffection in childhood a key contributing factor. The issues here identified were negative experiences of participation in Sunday school, competition for time provoked by other leisure pursuits and lack of quality conversation around questions of faith in the family.[15]

Not coincidentally, this period saw a steady rise in the deployment of employed youth ministers and the growth of a new

---

[13] Peter Brierley, *Reaching and Keeping Teenagers* (Tunbridge Wells/London: MARC/Christian Research, 1993).

[14] Peter Brierley, *Reaching and Keeping Tweenagers: Analysis of the 2001 Rakes Survey* (London: Christian Research, 2002).

[15] See Peter Brierley, 'One Generation from Extinction!', in *The Tide Is Running Out*, 93–132. This evidence is backed up by David Day and Philip May, *Teenage Beliefs* (Oxford: Lion, 1991).

subculture of Christian movements such as Soul Survivor Festival. In the mid-2000s hope emerged that this 'haemorrhaging of young people' might be abating: there was still decline but it had lessened and in some quarters of the Church signs of growth were beginning to become apparent.[16] This hopeful trend has become one of the key narratives in analysing statistical data on church attendance and affiliation. *From Anecdote to Evidence* merely resets this data into a more positive narrative of 'signs of growth'. Yet what lies behind this growth is the statistical data that shows that every generation is becoming less and less religious (in belief, attendance and affiliation).[17] One of the sociologists involved in the *Anecdote to Evidence* research, David Voas, has done extensive work with colleagues in this area. In one of their studies they have highlighted how decline in religious belief is not merely a general effect that happens across the population, but an observable trend of generational decline:

> Regular attendance (i.e. active belonging) is relatively easy to analyze. If neither parent attends at least once a month the chances of a child doing so are negligible: less than 3 percent. If both parents attend at least monthly, there is a 46 percent chance that the child will do so ... the trend does not depend on marriage patterns: the net effect is the same whether they are married or not.[18]

According to Voas and Crockett the Church has a half-life of one generation because in their view there is 'a failure in religious socialization [resulting] in whole generations being less active and less believing than the ones that came before'.[19]

---

[16] Brierley, *Pulling Out of the Nosedive*.

[17] In support of their claims, it is worth noting that similar patterns are now being established in North America; see David Kinnaman and Aly Hawkins, *You Lost Me: Why Young Christians Are Leaving Church – and Rethinking Faith* (Grand Rapids, MI: Baker, 2011).

[18] David Voas and Alasdair Crockett, 'Religion in Britain: Neither Believing nor Belonging', *Sociology* 39, no. 1 (1 February 2005): 11–28 (21). The chance of a child with one attending parent continuing to do so is 28 per cent, independent of the gender of the parent.

[19] Voas and Crockett, 'Religion in Britain', 20.

The Church's main problem for a number of years has been and remains an inability to pass on the faith to future generations and a growing disconnection between new generations who have no connection at all with church. One of the key priorities that the Church faces – including most if not all denominations – is in actually growing the number of young adults coming into faith.

This challenge is what I call a 'pastoral-mission task'. It is first and foremost a challenge to the way in which we perceive pastoral ministry to young people who have been brought up to believe. The evidence of a half-life of one generation suggests that pastoral ministry for young people within the Church requires an additional dimension. Voas and Crockett name this challenge as the *proximal impact of secularization*. By this they mean that trends in decline are not seen as constant across generations, but are identifiably felt between generations. As I will discuss later, there is something about the transition period of youth and young adulthood where the pressures of holding faith in a secular age are felt more keenly, or have a more profound effect. This dimension may well be the key understanding to help explain the identification of and the weakness in parental attitudes towards intentionally passing on faith. It also means that pastoral care of young people is in many contexts better considered as a task of pastoral mission – we are seeking to pass on the Christian faith into a new context.

In terms of impact on the health and growth of the Church this pastoral-mission task is well summarized by Voas and Crockett: 'decline in church attendance has not happened because many adults have stopped going to church. It is because more and more adults never start attending in the first place.'[20]

Addressing this challenge is one aspect of this urgent action. There is also, however, a second challenge in mission. If we think again about the trends in growth among young people these remain remarkably small. According to Voas and Crockett there is only a minimal chance (between 0.3 and 3 per cent depending

---

[20] *From Anecdote to Evidence*, 25.

on surveys) of a young person whose family are religiously non-affiliated becoming a Christian. In this context the parents of these young people appear to make little conscious attempt to pass on their non-religious worldviews.[21] Yet young people here are almost 100 per cent likely to adopt a similar non-religious worldview. The engagement then in mission remains minimal, but vital. This pastoral-mission task is one that has to address how such young people might be encouraged to explore faith and then hold to this faith in a context where this is not, for many, a naturally supported choice. This is a pattern which has, though, been with us in Europe, Canada and Australia for some time and is increasingly observable in the USA.

Faith in transition: responding to decline

News of young people leaving the Church is not new. It is an issue that the Church has been wrestling with for some time. Historically we can see the rise of youth-focused initiatives in the Victorian era, and in the Sunday school movement that predates even those. The Boys' Brigade, the YMCA and the Children's Special Service Mission each sought in the mid to late 1800s to find ways to engage and re-engage with children and young people who had ceased to 'attend' church. The idea of youth work to promote evangelism and discipleship and a more 'messy' form of church to engage young people who had ceased to attend Sunday schools after confirmation is an invention of the 1860s! In the early 1900s, particularly in evangelical circles, a deliberate focus on working with young people and young leaders emerged in the work of the Inter-Varsity Fellowship and Crusaders. Moving into the 1920s and beyond, the Church began to develop diverse provision for young people. This involved groups that were particular to denominations whose focus was on Bible study and prayer as well as some social activities; interdenominational societies that were not affiliated to a denomination but affirmed faith; and open clubs

---

[21] David Voas, 'Children and Youth Ministry and Church Growth', *Praxeis* 1, no. 1 (2014): 3–8 (4).

that were hosted or run by churches but didn't have any religious observance. In the 1940s this accounted for much of the youth work in the UK. Important though this provision has been, by the 1950s there was growing recognition that these approaches were still not responding to the changing patterns and beliefs of teenagers. It is well recognized that significant changes in attitudes to religion were seen in the period following the Second World War. The story in the USA is similar in many ways to this, but in the UK and much of Europe the impact on declining churchgoing has been more pronounced.

The continued disaffiliation of young people from churches from the 1950s onwards met with some new responses. At first there was a resurgence of youth fellowship movements and camps, and of so-called 'frontier work' with young people in mainly urban contexts who had little connection with the Church at all. More recent youth ministry provision has largely continued these trends and is recognizable across denominations. One facet of this has been the growth in 'full-timers' employed within church contexts as youth ministers or pastors, and a growth in equivalent posts in Christian youth organizations.

The call to action, then, is one that has been voiced for some time. Why it is more urgent now rests on two main reasons. First we are now in a position where actual attendance and affiliation is critically low. As we noted earlier, those churches having fewer than five young people can literally be said to have no future. Second, however, we have begun to change our understanding of what this 'drift from' the Church really means with respect to its long-term impact. These changes help to shape our response because they lead us to accept more fully what the underlying issues are that we need to address. In the main, we have seen these to be a drift from the Church as an institution, a rise in alternative or open spirituality, and more recent awareness of changes in perception of holding Christian faith. While in the past these changes have often been tackled in isolation from one another, they are perhaps better now considered as a composite challenge – they are the factors present in the proximal impact of secularization.

Believing without belonging: the changing place of religion

What constitutes 'a religion' or makes someone 'religious' is not actually easy to define. Understanding what constitutes a religion changes as the practices associated with this area of human life change.[22] Religion, though, gives a sense of institutional connection, authority and activity. To talk about young people's dissociation from religion is to discuss their disassociation from an institution, a recognized world faith or a set of organized practices. The first consideration about the changing nature of young people's faith centres on seeing the Church as an institution, and the problem as one of institutional decline. The phrase that captures this understanding is 'believing without belonging'.

The 'believing without belonging' thesis is associated with the sociologist Grace Davie, and has been a strong influence on understanding decline – or disaffiliation from church – for some time. Sociologists of religion noted that, with good reason, while people stopped attending church they still held some positive attitudes towards faith and religion. They still identified as being Christian on census surveys even if they were no longer even nominal churchgoers. This 'vicarious faith' was prevalent in Europe in particular and seen as a direct result of secularization – the fact that these countries were becoming more and more secular in outlook. This view is challenged in data related to that in *From Anecdote to Evidence* because it shows much more clearly that this is no longer the case.[23] Instead, decline in 'attendance' is now understood as a decline in 'belief, attendance and affiliation'.[24]

---

[22] Elisabeth Arweck and James A. Beckford, 'Social Perspectives', in *Religion and Change in Modern Britain*, ed. Linda Woodhead and Rebecca Catto (London/New York: Routledge, 2012), 352–72 (354).

[23] Voas and Crockett, 'Religion in Britain', 12. Challenging the thesis associated with Grace Davie, *Europe: The Exceptional Case: Parameters of Faith in the Modern World*, Sarum Theological Lectures (London: Darton, Longman & Todd, 2002).

[24] A. Crockett and D. Voas, 'Generations of Decline: Religious Change in 20th-Century Britain', *Journal for the Scientific Study of Religion* 45, no. 4 (2006): 567–84 (567).

The impact of these insights is important in two ways. First, the 'believing but not belonging' thesis helped to shore up the notion that if young people left the Church there was a likelihood that they might come back, especially when they in adult life had families of their own. The need for urgent action in such a circumstance is not as grave. Combined with the view that as part of their transition into adulthood young people might need to leave the Church in order to help establish their own identity, this influence led to the sense that what we had to do in work with children and young people was to 'give them a good start' – through church and school education – to help form them as well-rounded individuals with some sense of belief and this would be enough to provide the seeds of faith for later life.[25]

The pattern this led to in church life was one of accepting transition – young people would probably leave and this was 'normal'. Where there was action to engage with young people it was framed around institutional concerns or making church more 'attractive'. In the first instance, if young people are not participating in the Church as institution then this could be addressed by setting up better ways for them to be represented, locally and nationally, in church life. Denominations then have put great effort into youth councils, area youth officers and young people's representatives on synods. If the pressure to leave is one that is not primarily concerned with a 'drift from faith but a drift from church', then if we can make the experience of being in church better this drifting might be delayed. Young people have increased choices of activities and if church is 'dull' – well, let's not make it dull. Similarly, if young people need 'space' from parental influence then providing separate activities and specific youth events and organizations would be a way of 'reaching and keeping' such young people. Both of these strategies remain part of what churches are actually seeking to do now to prevent decline. While increased

---

[25] Harold Loukes, *Teenage Religion: An Enquiry into Attitudes and Possibilities among British Boys and Girls in Secondary Modern Schools* (London: SCM Press, 1961), published on behalf of the Institute of Christian Education; William K. Kay and Leslie J. Francis, *Drift from the Churches: Attitude toward Christianity during Childhood and Adolescence*, Religion, Culture and Society (Cardiff: University of Wales Press, 1996).

participation of young people in church life and leadership is of course welcome, and changing patterns of church to be more accessible are also welcome, these have minimal impact because the problem of decline is not merely institutional.

Spiritual but not religious: the shifting nature of belief

A second approach to understanding the problem of decline is captured in the phrase 'spiritual, not religious'. Again this is based on strong evidence of changing attitudes towards religion in secular pluralist societies. This moves the issue from one of institutional disconnection to a dislocation from organized religion itself, often accompanied by a desire to embrace and explore other spiritual and religious traditions. This attitude is captured by comments from young people such as those that Phil Rankin interviewed in his book *Buried Spirituality*: 'Religion has been such a negative force in the world. I believe there's a God, but I'd never go to church again. Christians only make it harder to see God, to experience things.'[26]

Here there was not just an institutional disconnection, but a feeling that religious belief was problematic – this being perceived as either hypocritical, superficial or unnecessary. This finding is borne out by work in the sociology of religion that has identified that many people consider themselves to be 'spiritual but not religious'.[27] The pastoral-mission challenge in this context becomes one of meeting this 'need'.

These views seem to suggest that young people possess a sense of spiritual hunger – disaffiliation is a sign of disappointment. In this situation the Church ought to respond with greater clarity about its own spirituality, be this catholic, charismatic or alternative. The rise of contemplative prayer, Taizé and other youth-focused prayer and worship activities illustrate this.[28] Similarly, more

---

[26] A young person's view of religion in Phil Rankin, *Buried Spirituality: A Report on the Findings of the Fellowship in the Spirituality of Young People Based at Sarum College, Salisbury* (Salisbury: Sarum College Press, 2005), 52.

[27] Paul Heelas and Linda Woodhead, *The Spiritual Revolution: Why Religion Is Giving Way to Spirituality*, Religion in the Modern World (Malden, MA/Oxford: Blackwell, 2005).

[28] Mark Yaconelli, *Contemplative Youth Ministry* (London: SPCK, 2006).

youth-focused approaches might well seek to openly address spiritual questions and help young people to explore their inchoate spirituality.[29] Such approaches, like those to fostering participation, are not without merit but do not prove to be all that is required. It is important in our context of the pastoral-mission task to understand what is perceived about being spiritual and how this might be held as distinct from what Christians mean by spirituality – to talk of this as the centre of faith, not religion. Here the research conducted among young people by Mayo-Collins and team is important. In assessing the 'faith of Generation Y' the members of this team talk of 'spirituality' as more akin to a human capacity, one linked to a sense of wonder, or dread, and an awareness of our relational connectedness to the world and others.

However, there is a distinction to be made between this capacity – what these authors call *formative spirituality* – and an active spirituality where a person is consciously exploring this sense of wonder and connectedness. This *transformative spirituality* is connected to deepening an appreciation of this sense of 'transcendence' through deliberate engagement in religious, or non-religious, practices. For these authors a key problem is that they feel many young people no longer regard the Church as a source of transformative spirituality.[30]

Making sense of the worldview of young people requires a conscious shift to appreciate how and where they find meaning and how and where they express what is sacred to them. In the research on which *Making Sense of Generation Y* is based, young people show that the primary place from which they draw meaning is popular culture and that the things that are most sacred to them are their family and friends. This worldview does not gravitate towards large meta-narratives – overarching accounts of meaning that might be present in religion or politics. It is a 'here and now worldview rather than one that looks to something beyond'.

[29] Maxine Green and Chandu Christian, *Accompanying Young People on Their Spiritual Quest* (London: National Society/Church House Publishing, 1998).

[30] Sara B. Savage, Sylvia Collins-Mayo and Bob Mayo, *Making Sense of Generation Y: The World View of 15- to 25-Year-Olds*, Explorations (London: Church House Publishing, 2006), 12–13.

Within this, the notion of 'happiness' is held highly. Happiness is both a goal and an attitude; self-fulfilment in experiences and positive relationships are prized; being 'carefree' or 'happy-go-lucky' is an attitude that helps sustain you in life.[31] While this assessment of young people's worldview cannot be exhaustive, it does tally with findings from other research on these crucial points. Family and friends are important because in the 'here and now' these people provide the closest notion of something held as sacred – something that you could not do without. They are also the people who essentially support this so-called 'happy midi' worldview. There is in this worldview little or no need for spirituality as many religious traditions would perceive it. These are significant shifts. If young people do remain connected to church and do still identify as holding to Christian faith this too, however, is not immune from change. Spirituality is shifting, but as I discuss next, so too is the way young people perceive and talk about faith.

Faithful with ambivalence: the diminishing presence of faith

The third area of transition is within understandings of the Christian faith itself. Given the changes that we have seen in institutional disaffiliation and the move towards open spirituality among young people, it should perhaps be obvious that within Christian practice we might see similar transitions. These transitions in approach to faith are captured by the respondents' view on prayer in *The Faith of Generation Y*, the follow-up research to *Making Sense of Generation Y*:

> If you're struggling – everyone struggles in life – sometimes you need someone. Even though you have got your family and friends to talk to, it sometimes just feels like you need somebody else to talk to, so you talk to God.[32]

This comment captures the sense of faith itself shifting to become part of the 'happy midi-narrative' frame that young people inhabit.

---

[31] Savage et al., *Making Sense of Generation Y*, 38.
[32] Sylvia Collins-Mayo, Bob Mayo, Sally Nash and Christopher Cocksworth, *The Faith of Generation Y* (London: Church House Publishing, 2010), 49.

This change is best identified in work from North America from the large and detailed National Study of Youth and Religion. The findings from this are summarized by the lead author Christian Smith as a recognizable approach to religion – mainly Christian – among young people as Moral Therapeutic Deism (MTD). This asserts that young people see faith as being about trying to be good people (Moral), that God is essentially there to make us feel good or solve our problems (Therapeutic), but such a God is not largely involved in our affairs otherwise (Deism).[33] While this captures something of the particular religious culture of North America, it is a description that fits well for the challenge of forming faith in a secular age for any young person.

Such a shift is understandable given the transitions we have noted. First, a Christian faith that is reducible to 'being a good person' is more plausible than one that requires a transformative spirituality located in the external authority of the Bible, the Church or a personal relationship with God. It is a choice that fits with a secular humanist age. Similarly, the idea of a God who is held at a distance – as an impersonal deity there when we need it but not demanding anything of us – is a more comfortably held view in a secular age. This is a God whom we can trust to pray towards without any assured sense of presence. We can genuinely pray in hope, but not run too much risk in being disappointed when we do not 'feel' or see a reply! This is a God who fits with formative spirituality, discussed earlier. Faith in God is not seen as transformative. The transcendent nature of God is 'flattened'; the expectation of a reply to such prayers that might demand a response from the person praying is lessened. The third factor – faith as 'therapeutic' – speaks to the 'use' of faith. Here, there is strong resonance with the findings of the traits of spirituality in the happy midi-narrative discussed earlier. God is there for our happiness. Yet the challenge is perhaps to see how such 'use' might be harnessed. If faith doesn't have a 'purchase' – a 'use' in life – then what would

---

[33] Christian Smith and Melinda Lundquist Denton, *Soul Searching: The Religious and Spiritual Lives of American Teenagers* (Oxford/New York: Oxford University Press, 2005).

make a person want to seek this as part of a transformative spirituality?

A subsequent reflection on this pattern from Kenda Dean is also pertinent to the story we have in *From Anecdote to Evidence*. Not only are we seeing generational decline in faith, but a transition to a 'weaker' form of faith – one where only 38 per cent of committed Christian parents see it as being 'important' to be proactive in passing on faith to the next generation. In considering MTD, Dean argues that this is the faith young people have because it is the faith their parents have. This is our faith. Maybe the ambivalent faith shown by parents is a symptom of a wider holding of an MTD-like faith in the UK context. This means then that in the pastoral-mission context we should not make assumptions about the depth of formation of young people we assume to have been 'brought up to believe'. This does mean that the pastoral-mission challenge of faith formation is rightly set across all generations. In fact it may be that it is only when the time comes for adult believers to consciously think about passing on faith to children and young people that they themselves become aware of the shape of their own faith. This raises key questions about how youth ministry, and more keenly family ministry, responds. A second issue, though, lies in how the traits of MTD are specifically worked with so that they might be more critically seen as a reliable faith – a Christian faith that is fit for use in a secular age. In both of these instances, then, there is a crucial aspect of youth ministry as a place to affirm and enable the indwelling of the tradition we are seeking to pass on.

This very brief survey of the changing nature of religion, spirituality and faith among young people reveals the factors in holding faith in a secular age that influence young people's faith formation and affect the transmission of faith between generations. As identified in *From Anecdote to Evidence* it is a failure in transmission of faith in these transitions that is occurring; this is the proximal impact of secularization. As individuals begin to move from childhood to adult faith – or consider faith for the first time as young adults – there are challenges to faith that become barriers or blocks to faith formation. These can be summarized as choice, sense and use. In *choice* there is the decline in religious participation and the number of other worldview options. In *sense* there is the challenge of making sense of formative or transformative spiritualities in a context where the dominant frame is a here-and-now happy midi-narrative. In *use* the challenge is one of how young people respond to making faith a transformative part of their lives – not by co-opting God into the end goal of happiness alone. These will be the three themes I will consider in richer detail when I look at the views and insights of the young people I talked to about their faith and the role of youth ministry within this. These are the three principal challenges we are urged to take action to counter. However, to close this chapter, I want to affirm that investment in growth is not merely about stemming decline; it is also about addressing the challenge of faith formation so that future generations of faith are part of fruitful, growing communities of faith.

Faith in growth: investing in youth ministry

The importance of forming faith in teenage years has been highlighted in a number of studies over the years. In 1992, John Finney showed clear data that most people who are Christians today took the decision to become Christians in teenage years.[34] This is especially true for those who were not raised in a Christian family. This story continues to be supported by more recent data and has long been held as an argument for investing in work to nurture and form faith in this time of life. Yet the changing patterns around religion, belief and faith above beg the question of what we actually mean by faith formation; what are we aiming towards in seeking this outcome for young people?

When we consider faith formation – and the failure of transmission – we need to be very careful that we are not implying that what is needed is for young people to adopt a carbon copy of the

---

[34] John Finney, *Finding Faith Today: How Does It Happen?* (Swindon: British and Foreign Bible Society, 1992). See also *Report from the Archbishops' Evangelism Task Group*, GS 2015 (London: The General Synod of the Church of England, 2016), 11.

faith that they see and experience from previous generations. Similarly, if we are critical of the way in which previous generations have adopted an approach to faith that does not seem to have the weight that might be wished for in the Christian tradition, there is something also in the task of faith formation that aims towards the renewal of the Church. The tension here is clear. What is the balance between inheriting and evolving faith?

I use the term 'faith' rather than 'belief' or 'religion' deliberately. It is faith that we are looking to see grow, not churches. It is faith we are hoping to help young people form, not beliefs or religious views. Faith has several characteristics that are important in this regard. First, from a Christian perspective it is about the orientation and outworking of relationship between a person – or community – and God. Second, faith also speaks of a social dimension to being Christian. It puts us closer to the idea of 'lived religion' – the way in which young people actually live out their religion – and the way in which this religious identity shapes their understanding of who they are and their interactions with others around them.[35] Finally, faith does say something about beliefs – about the tenets of these beliefs and the practices through which we learn and express them.

The theologian and Christian educator Edward Farley describes faith as the 'Christian habitus'. Farley uses 'habitus' to mean an understanding of mind and orientation of the soul, 'a knowledge of God and of what God reveals'.[36] How this happens is a topic of discussion more frequently associated with ministerial formation, but it is an equally valid issue for Christian formation. Habitus is often used to describe a depth of faith but also a capacity to act faithfully. We develop this attitude and ability as an outcome of 'gift and work'. Faith is something that we understand theologically to be a gift of God, to be something that we cannot generate but that is generated within us by the Spirit of

---

[35] Nicola Madge, Peter J. Hemming, Kevin Stenson and Nick Allum, *Youth on Religion: The Development, Negotiation and Impact of Faith and Non-Faith Identity* (Hove/New York: Routledge, 2014).

[36] Edward Farley, *Theologia: The Fragmentation and Unity of Theological Education* (Philadelphia: Fortress Press, 1983), 35.

God. This emphasis on gift, though, belies the fact that faith is also work.[37]

The educationalist John Westerhoff argues that faith captures an important relational aspect of believing that religion can often, even subconsciously, sideline. For Westerhoff, 'we can know about religion, but we live in faith'. Further, 'Faith can be inspired within a community of faith but it cannot be given to one person by another. Faith is expressed, transformed, and made meaningful by persons sharing their faith in an historic, tradition-bearing community.'[38]

When we look at the reasons why young people disconnect from church, we need to do so in relation to how this does or does not affect their sense of connection to the historic Christian faith and the various expressions of this today. We are also interested, though, in whether being part of a church has any real effect on young people in regard to 'transforming' their sense of who they are. For this to occur you need to have a particular community within which there is both the trust and the time to engage with the Christian tradition and Church to facilitate this. I am aware that others see this as less of a requirement in how we might engage young people in their sense of spirituality and understanding of the world. I am open to the possibility of God meeting with and becoming known by young people away from the institutional Church, but I will mainly argue that Christian faith has to be connected in a clear way to Christianity as 'lived religion' and that this is generated by our participation in a 'community of persons sharing faith' – though is not reducible to this.[39]

This links to the third aspect of faith highlighted, namely that this 'community of faith sharers' is a tradition-bearing community. As I will discuss later, a key contention in this book is that the task of being Christian is an active one and that 'church' is the place and people where this task is primarily located. One of the

---

[37] Farley, *Theologia*, 44.

[38] John H. Westerhoff, *Will Our Children Have Faith?* rev. edn (Harrisburg, PA: Morehouse, 2000), 19.

[39] Gerrit Immink, *Faith: A Practical Theological Reconstruction*, Studies in Practical Theology (Grand Rapids, MI/Cambridge: Eerdmans, 2005), 19–20.

founding figures in contemporary practical theology and Christian education, James Fowler, describes this challenge as 'enacting Christian presence'. This includes being not only a tradition-bearing community, but also one that responds to 'an unfolding future, with instincts and imaginations shaped by memories of God's faithful action in the past, and experiences of God in the present'.[40] Following into the future is the task of the Church as a whole, yet youth ministry is perhaps particularly and crucially positioned within this corporate activity.

In seeking to understand how young people's faith is formed and expressed we have to pay closer attention to their experience of the Christian faith as 'lived religion' – what it is like for them to be Christian in the current context. We have to look at how they engage in 'transformative spirituality' – where the faith sharing with other Christians and the experience of God through Christian practices is transformative in shaping their sense of self and place in the world. Finally we have to not only see this as a means by which young people are formed, but also see how their participation in church helps form the people of God following into the future. This is the faith we are seeking for our children and young people to grow into. This is faith generation. In the next chapter I will look at how youth ministry is ideally set to help to foster and form such faith.

Questions for discussion

1 Given the trends highlighted in the section on growth and decline, how has your church experienced these? For future reference do you consider your church to be:

   (a) a church with a small base – fewer than five young people;

   (b) a church with a medium base – around a dozen children and young people;

   (c) a church with a firm base – at least two distinct groups for children and young people.

---

[40] James W. Fowler, 'The Emerging New Shape of Practical Theology', in *Practical Theology: International Perspectives*, ed. Friedrich Schweitzer and Johannes A. van der Ven, Erfahrung und Theologie, Bd 340172-1135 (Frankfurt am Main/New York: P. Lang, 1999), 75–92 (82).

2 What examples or anecdotes do you have of your own around the changing approaches to religion, spirituality and faith highlighted in this chapter?

3 Ask the young people you work with or live with what faith means to them; how does this compare to the sketch summarized here and to your own views?

4 Choose one young person you know, and commit to pray for them every day for a week.

2

Youth ministry and the urgent task of faith generation

————◆·◆·◆————

Christianity is a way of life that emerges from a particular
perception of life in general and in our own lives in
particular . . . 'Christians', wrote Tertullian, the third-
century theologian, 'are made, not born.' The question
then, as now, is how?   *(John Westerhoff[1])*

If we are to address the failure of faith transmission, we have to
ask why the time of youth is particularly susceptible to the impact
of secularization. Faith formation, as I briefly mentioned earlier,
is a complex account of our development as human beings in
relation to God and the community of faith. Understanding how
young people form and express faith needs to take into account the
influence of family and the wider community of faith. As a process
of 'gift and work' there is also a personal response that relates to
the way in which an individual young person may or may not accept,
seek or receive faith. In the same way, a young person might also
want, work at and hope to have faith, but for any number of
reasons not see this materialize in a tangible way. The role of youth
ministry is to nurture the gift of faith and support the work of
faith among young people. This can take a number of forms. It
is important, though, because it seeks to address specifically the
challenges to faith formation discussed in the previous chapter.

   To begin to look at how investment in youth ministry can help
faith generation, it is vital to identify what this area of pastoral-
mission activity is and what it involves. The positive influence

---

[1] John H. Westerhoff, 'A Call to Catechesis', *The Living Light* 14, no. 3 (1977), 354–8 (354).

that youth ministry has on growth in *From Anecdote to Evidence* was observed in sampled churches that had clear youth ministry activity – around a fifth of the total sample: 'There is a particularly strong association between growth and youth programmes. Youth retreats, conferences or camps ... [of churches offering these], exactly three quarters report growth, versus exactly half among the others.'[2]

In this chapter I want to begin to unpack how this association might be seen as something more substantive – as causation. It is true that in growing churches there is likely to be the need for provision of some kind for young people – a simple explanation of the association with growth. In beginning to get into the substance of this practice we can see that there is also the strong likelihood that what is being undertaken is helpful in addressing the challenges of the proximal impact of secularization.

While there will of course be diversity of opinion and disagreement over the role of youth ministry as one element of the Church's response to faith generation, it is helpful to begin by reflecting on what we have learnt through the past five decades of this activity. This learning is important because, however you conceive of it, youth ministry has been at the forefront of the Church's response to the proximal impact of secularization for at least the past 50 years and, depending on how one views its earliest forms, for perhaps considerably longer.

Youth ministry has been a key way in which the Church has sought to respond to the challenge of forming faith in the modern age. Whether one looks at youth ministry in Catholic or Protestant traditions, all denominations have to some extent adopted patterns of practice where work with young people in discipleship and mission has some form of focused activity or specialized practice.[3] In my view, it is no coincidence that where we see this work being supported by a paid worker there are

---

[2] *From Anecdote to Evidence: Findings from the Church Growth Research Programme 2011–13* (London: The Church of England, 2014), 26.

[3] Pete Ward and Lindsay Urwin, eds, *Youthful Spirit* (London: Tufton Books/The Church Union, 1998).

signs of growth; this is an indication that there is a focus and coordination to this activity. Given this, it is not necessarily the specific employment of a worker that is the crucial issue, but that in making such an appointment the church is signalling that this focus is a priority. The activity of youth ministry can be summarized as a combination of Christian education, cross-cultural mission and contextual pastoral care. These approaches are identifiable with specific periods in the development of youth ministry. More important from a current perspective is that each approach has laid down key priorities that influence the way we undertake youth ministry in most contexts today. These are *distinctive learning, intentional relationships* and *transformational practices*. By looking at these overlapping functions we can begin to see how youth ministry has been instrumental in the Church's response to forming faith in the modern age. However, this is not to say that there are not new things to learn.

Forming faith in the modern age: youth ministry as contribution to the challenge

We only have youth ministry because of the modern world. This is the view that Andrew Root proposes in his discussion of the development of youth ministry in the USA. Youth ministry has come about in church practice in line with young people becoming a 'category' in society.[4] Teenagers are a marketable group for the economy and have distinct cultural and leisure pursuits. Young people are the recipients of education and are expected to attend these institutions rather than work with their families. In fact in many ways the Church has aided this change, especially through its involvement in education. This connection is important because it helps to identify that the way in which we have sought to help young people form faith is deeply connected to their being, and becoming, modern young adults. This has led to some necessary interventions into how faith is explored and expressed – and

---

[4] Andrew Root, *Revisiting Relational Youth Ministry: From Strategy of Influence to a Theology of Incarnation* (Downer's Grove, IL: IVP, 2007).

some unforeseen consequences. These interventions connect to the changing place in society for children and young people and also to how the Church has tried to respond to the transitions in faith discussed in the previous chapter.

Youth ministry as Christian education: providing distinctive learning

There is a common pattern in the UK and North America which connects the origins of youth ministry with the modern 'invention' of the adolescent and then the teenager. This is linked in the main to the development of education: first with the Church's involvement in this provision as part of its mission and, second, with the need to adapt church provision to begin to meet the needs of this emerging segment of the population.

Initially church work with children and young people involved mission-focused activities to provide children with education, and to work to make welfare conditions more acceptable. This activity was, however, deeply connected to faith and undertaken in the assumption that this was how young people would be taught and formed. The Sunday school movement is the exemplar of this and in many ways set a template for the way in which the Church organized its response to young people. The Church in many contexts has undertaken teaching young people to read and teaching them the faith at the same time for over a hundred years. This educational activity merged ancient traditions of catechesis – the teaching of the faith – into new approaches that involved separate Bible studies and classes for young people and special services for children.[5] This modern phenomenon of the nineteenth century has left a strong influence in that the approach of education is at the heart of Christian work with young people.

The development of this activity in the UK and many parts of Europe was distinct from that in North America. In the USA it was the local church's responsibility to school young people in the faith, supported by 'public' schooling that would uphold

---

[5] Pete Ward, *Growing up Evangelical: Youthwork and the Making of a Subculture* (London: SPCK, 1996), 27.

religion as culturally important. In the UK and Europe, historically because of the Church's role in education, the teaching of the faith was seen as a core activity of schools until only very recently. In the 1950s and 1960s there was growing recognition that confessional 'religious education' in schools was failing to achieve the desired aim of providing an understanding and experience of Christianity.[6] This provoked a dual focus in approaches to faith and education. One strand focused on enhanced training and institutional support in teaching religious education. Another saw an increased emphasis on formal 'Christian education' within churches.

In formal education the distinction between teaching *about* and teaching *into* faith became much clearer in the 1960s and 1970s. More formal approaches were taken up by many denominations with focused work to provide resources and training for those teaching the faith in church settings.[7] An important aspect of this was the emphasis placed on the value of critical learning – helping young people to develop self-awareness and the capacity to openly adopt a faith of their own.[8] Even in the more informal setting of youth fellowships the task of teaching followed a strong cultural pattern, as highlighted later when Aiken describes a youth minister's primary role as 'to be as colourful and imaginative as we can [in teaching] young people to have a real understanding of what it means to be a Christian'.[9] This remains evident in the number of resources that youth ministers still draw upon to support 'teaching', including ideas for video clips, analogies and topics of teaching that address issues perceived to be of concern to young people, or topics that are a concern because they might be negative

---

[6] Harold Loukes, *Teenage Religion: An Enquiry into Attitudes and Possibilities among British Boys and Girls in Secondary Modern Schools* (London: SCM Press, 1961).

[7] Martin Wellings and Andrew Wood, 'Facets of Formation: Theology through Training', in *Unmasking Methodist Theology*, ed. Clive Marsh (New York/London: Continuum, 2004), 70–83 (71).

[8] David Heywood, 'Theology or Social Science? The Theoretical Basis for Christian Education', in *The Contours of Christian Education*, ed. Jeff Astley and David Day (Great Wakering: McCrimmons, 1992), Chapter 7.

[9] Nick Aiken, *Working with Teenagers: The Essential Handbook*, new rev. edn (London: Marshall Pickering, 1994), 29–30.

influences on young people, as well as a significant number of resources that focus on 'Christian basics'.

At the same time as developing this focus and resourcing for work in youth groups, the understanding of the role that the whole faith community plays in forming faith has become more prevalent in formal educational models as applied in Sunday schools and church-based education. This is seen clearly in the work of John Westerhoff and his enculturation model. In the 1970s Westerhoff proposed a developmental model of faith formation that stressed that *all* persons of faith experience some form of conversion to their faith. He regards this as a necessary experience of conversion which is best understood as a radical turning from *faith given* to *faith owned*. Enculturation describes the way in which church communities can foster this ownership through a *deliberate socialization* into the community of faith and its practices. This is the type of Christian education through which a child or young person can best form a personal Christian identity. Westerhoff's model was proposed in part to redress a bias towards schooling models of Christian education that he felt could not provide for the necessary community of faith to form; a focus on teaching in separate youth groups is particularly open to such a critique. However, this approach depends on there being a broader 'ecology of faith' where 'Sunday school' served to nurture faith that was also sustained by the town, the family, the public school and popular religious culture – all joining to support the formation of personal faith.

An alternative approach to connecting faith formation with formal education also emerged in this period. This stressed the need to develop informal education with young people around faith in youth work settings, which in the 1950s was being put on a statutory footing alongside schooling. This Christian youth work focused activity on the increasing numbers of young people disconnected from church, especially in towns and cities. Approaches to informal education were pioneered by those connected with 'frontier' Christian youth work. In this mode youth ministry was seen as being best fulfilled by a professional youth worker who worked alongside clergy and volunteers in providing church-based youth work activities. These were predominantly focused on work with young people in inner-city environments, particularly those where there was an existing 'mission hall' or 'settlement'. These establishments, such as the Mayflower Centre in east London and the Salmon Centre in south London, were established by university Christian Unions to promote mission in urban, industrial areas. 'Informal education' as understood in this youth work context does not refer to the informal socialization processes that Westerhoff signifies, but to a style of education that relies on encouraging learning from experience, with a commitment to move young people from 'dependence to independence' and to enable them to 'reflect upon and be responsible for their own actions'.[10] This task, Ellis suggests, is not contrary to the approach of those who might seek to simply call young people to adopt faith (in evangelism, for instance), but requires a fuller view of the faith to which young people are being called, and Ellis argues that Jesus' primary teaching style was that of the informal educa-tor – using stories, physical location and objects, and reflection upon experience as patterns in his teaching.

More latterly – from the late 1990s – youth work approaches have also influenced the way in which informal education is used in youth ministry contexts within churches. This is articu-lated by Brierley, for instance, who suggests that 'education' is best conceived of in the context of small groups within which workers can help to foster community and enable young people to develop social and communication skills. Brierley argues that informal education in group work enables young people to 'meet together for a fixed period of time to consider the authenticity of the Christian faith'. In such a context young people learn more from conversation and having fun together than they might in attempting to deliver similar material through 'formal teaching'.[11]

---

[10] John W. Ellis, 'Youth Work and Evangelism – Can They Co-Exist with Integrity?', *Perspectives: Journal of Reflective Youth Work Practice and Applied Theology* (Summer 1998): 10–12 (10).

[11] Danny Brierley, *Joined Up: An Introduction to Youthwork and Ministry*, Youthwork: The Resources (Going Deeper) (Carlisle: Authentic, 2003).

The importance of highlighting this journey and influence is that within any youth ministry context there are then a number of aspects of Christian education that are being attempted. Youth ministry groups are trying to provide places where there is to a greater or lesser degree a mixture of formal and informal Christian education aimed towards the task of catechesis – of helping to form and develop young people's understanding and ownership of faith. At the same time, youth ministry is also seeking to be part of a whole community approach to faith formation and to set this 'teaching' in a process of 'enculturation'. We are doing this because we recognize that this task does not 'naturally happen'. Making such 'teaching' relevant and enjoyable is part of this task, but not the primary aim. This is not a set of practices developed to help 'keep' young people by being entertaining – or at least should not be. We are doing it to provide opportunities for distinctive learning for young Christians – distinctive in that it addresses what the distinctive aspects of being Christian might be and distinctive in that it is provision for particular groups of young people. Such socialization and critical learning needs to be owned by the Church in order for faith to be owned by our young people.

Youth ministry as mission: forming intentional relationships

Mission has played a key role in the development of youth ministry. As noted above, early forms of practice – such as Sunday schools – were understood as mission activities. The frontier youth work based in informal education was similarly missional. In addition Christian mission organizations such as Youth for Christ and Youth with a Mission have since the 1940s and 1950s put on evangelistic activities and programmes for young people. These approaches paid attention to the ways in which the gospel might be better communicated and received if this was done through the use of popular culture and events. This work would develop into broader-based local projects seeking to engage young people not connected to the Church in youth-work style activities, with the purpose of also encouraging interest in the message of the Christian faith.

As this work developed, the missional approach to youth ministry began to be shaped by insights from mission studies into how this engagement might be more fulsomely approached. Such missional approaches to youth ministry see the task of enabling young people to form and express faith as a process often akin to the way in which the gospel is communicated across cultures (contextualization) and the way in which being church is appropriately formed within new cultures (indigenization). The issue of culture is not an intellectual exercise, but requires that the Christian youth worker does his or her theology 'on young people's turf'; contextualization is not the process of reflection upon culture, but the process of participating within young people's cultural worlds, through 'incarnational commitment and experience' and the contextualization of the gospel, requires workers to go and be with young people.[12] What differs in this approach from that of youth work described above is the centring of this task as one of inculturation of the gospel within youth cultures. This approach is strongly associated with the writing of Pete Ward.

Drawing on theory around youth subcultures, Ward argues that church-based youth ministry has a particular subculture and as such struggles to be suitable as a point of contextual mission within other youth subcultures.[13] Ward argues that this has become a barrier to mission, even though youth ministry youth groups provide for strong socialization of young people raised in church families. This type of activity has at its heart the formation of close relationships between young people in fellowship groups and with their leaders or workers. These groups remain missional in that there is an expectation that friends of these young people may also become involved in them. As such they operate a model of 'inside-out' growth where a nucleus of young people as the core group might grow through others joining.

---

[12] Mark H. Senter, Wesley Black, Chap Clark and Malan Nel, *Four Views of Youth Ministry and the Church: Inclusive Congregational, Preparatory, Missional, Strategic* (Grand Rapids, MI: Zondervan, 2001), 79.

[13] Pete Ward, *Youthwork and the Mission of God*, Frameworks for Relational Outreach (London: SPCK, 1997), 17.

A different approach to working with young people who are not connected to the Church is proposed as 'outside-in' work. This involves Christian youth workers (paid or unpaid) undertaking a process of relationally based activities as the means of connecting with young people and seeking ways in which the gospel can be contextually communicated. What is distinct in this approach from Christian education is a focus on the centrality of these relationships. It involves 'meeting young people where they're at', as the title of Richard Passmore's influential book on this style of work highlights.[14] Passmore draws on the informal education methods of youth work in advocating for the importance of connecting with young people in 'street spaces'. However, what is different from earlier informal education approaches in Christian youth work is that these tools are drawn upon for a specific aim. From a missional stance the aim of Christian youth work is for young people to participate in the worship of God. As Pete Ward asserts, this youth ministry away from the Church should enable young people to be able to 'express a form of worship and prayer which fits to their culture and day-to-day experience of God'.[15] This involves ways in which they might seek to utilize aspects of their own cultural style in worship as well as a necessity to engage and internalize aspects of church tradition with which they are not culturally familiar. Ward, along with others involved in this practice, recognizes that such expressions of the gospel ought not to be isolated entities but be linked to other expressions of church. It is 'outside-in' youth ministry. This, however, should be carefully built as this kind of work can often be 'subverted' – intentionally or otherwise – by church-based youth ministry to the extent that the process of contextualization is muted.

This missional youth ministry has also been termed 'incarnational' youth work as it is predicated on the ongoing presence of the youth worker with young people and a theological understanding

---

[14] Richard Passmore, Jo Pimlott and Nigel Pimlott, *Meet Them Where They're At: Helping Churches Engage Young People through Detached Youth Work* (Bletchley: Scripture Union, 2003).

[15] Pete Ward, 'Christian Relational Care', in *Relational Youthwork*, ed. Pete Ward (Oxford/ Sutherland, Australia: Lynx/Albatross Books, 1995), 13–40 (21–2).

around the incarnation.[16] Incarnation represents an act of boundary crossing, emulating the way in which Christ became known in culture. Incarnation represents any move to cross cultural boundaries in order that the gospel might become known in that context. This is not suggesting that workers should merely seek to 'act like Christ', but that they play a part in a process of Christ becoming known. Such boundary crossing enables workers to listen and learn; to discern and speak into a culture. It is also an act of intervention, a sign that God acts in his mission to come to be with us.[17] Given this centrality of incarnation, of bodily going, it is not surprising that the role of the worker is highlighted as significant in this process of contextualization. Relational youth work is an apt term for this approach, but it is the intentionality of these relationships that is important.

The appreciation of the impact that effective cultural expression might have on young people's faith formation from these missional perspectives has also been insightful and influential with respect to worship activities within church-based youth ministry. This recognizes that young people within Christian communities have cultural tastes and influences shaped by broader youth culture, which if 'used' in worship can be transformative.[18] While this attracts critique from some quarters around trapping worship in practices that are more akin to entertainment, studies have noted that such worship is profoundly influential. Steve Emery-Wright, through research with Methodist young people, highlights the fact that for many Christian young people the experience of such worship is essential for their sense of relationship with God.[19] In this sense the pastoral-mission task also includes some requirement for young people to contextualize worship into the cultures in which they participate. Research in Catholic youth ministry supports this, identifying similar importance to distinct

---

[16] For further theological understanding on this topic see Ward, *Youthwork and the Mission of God*, 43–68, and Root, *Revisiting Relational Youth Ministry*.

[17] Ward, *Youthwork and the Mission of God*, 14.

[18] Pete Ward, *Youth Culture and the Gospel* (London: Marshall Pickering, 1992).

[19] Steve Emery-Wright, *Passionate Worship: Hearing the Voices of Young People*, Monograph Series (Cambridge: YTC Press, 2009).

youth-worship spaces alongside – or incorporating – more traditional liturgy and worship.[20]

Youth ministry, then, has developed action that seeks to engage in pastoral-mission work in different ways with young people away from the Church and young people within the Church. The two styles, though, have connections and mutual influences such that these approaches carry with them many of the educational approaches to providing distinctive learning but also place intentional relationships at the heart of youth ministry practice. One involves growing groups and forming new connections through intentional Christian youth work, and the other focuses on forming intentional youth work relationships to enable groups of young people to explore understandings of the gospel. Both approaches place importance on intentional relationships and aim towards generating intentional relationship with God. The influence of this practice, while having its origins in evangelical youth work, has been significant across most denominations. This influence has been to affirm that to engage young people's spiritual interest and transformation requires the need to 'inculturate' the gospel into young people's cultural contexts.

Youth ministry as pastoral care: engaging transformational practices

Groups lie at the heart of youth ministry, whether this is traced through education or mission approaches. While both of these have particular perspectives around the educational merit of group work or the importance of working with young people's self-chosen peer groups in mission, the third approach I want to distinguish develops a different understanding of the purpose these groups might play. A pastoral approach in youth ministry seeks to situate understanding of the purpose of these groups within a broader tradition of pastoral theology and in particular to name and foster methods of working with young people that centre on 'Christian practices'. This has been influenced by youth ministry

---

[20] Avril Baigent, *The Y Church Report* (Northampton: Youth Office of the Roman Catholic Diocese, 2003).

approaches in 'mainline' North American contexts, but also connects with traditions in the UK that retain a clear importance of
traditional Christian practices and more contemplative traditions.

Two aspects of this understanding have been prevalent. The first
is that youth ministry ought to encourage intergenerational connection within church and that the role of the family as a primary
context for the nurture of faith ought also to be supported, not
circumvented, by youth ministry. The second is that youth ministry ought to be considered a pastoral collaboration between
young people, leaders, parents and the wider community that has
elements of intergenerational worship and relationship mixed with
distinct youth-focused space and practices.

Intergenerational approaches are advocated by Mark DeVries,
who argues that the pastoral action of youth ministry needs to
empower Christian parents to continue to relate to their children
through any changes in the dynamics of relationships that occur
in teenage years. Dean and Foster draw upon DeVries' view in
considering the importance of integrating youth ministry within
congregational life, considering that 'the Christian youth group is
notoriously unreliable for fostering on-going faith'[21] and suggesting it is because much practice is so isolated from the life of the
congregation that when young people leave the youth group, they
effectively leave the church. A similar view is offered in the UK
context by Jason Gardner. For Gardner, reconnecting adults and
young people is a central function of church because it is in these
relationships that young people can better consider what it means
to be an 'adult'. There is a 'generation gap' that is present within
contemporary culture but the Church is called to help bridge and
not reinforce this. Strong within Gardner's approach is an ethic
of 'hospitality' to welcome, support and nurture young people's
approaches to being Christian.[22] In considering the balance between
intergenerational and separated activities Mark Senter suggests
that the specialist youth minister is one leg of a three-legged stool,

---

[21] Kenda Creasy Dean and Ron Foster, *The Godbearing Life: The Art of Soul Tending for
Youth Ministry* (Nashville, TN: Upper Room Books, 1998), 30.
[22] Jason Gardner, *Mend the Gap: Can the Church Reconnect the Generations?* (Nottingham:
IVP, 2008).

the other two being family and community. The tension in this, as Senter points out, is that such a call to family-based ministry offers little support in defining what 'a family' ought to look like, and moreover how families should engage in actively encouraging and enabling young people to form faith.[23] All youth ministry activity is in some way attempting to merge and manage these tensions.

This first dimension of the pastoral approach is important because it helps to situate the larger community within which Christian practices are understood and interpreted – a similar process to understanding enculturation. What this approach also does, however, is focus on how engagement with Christian practices – worship, prayer, Communion, baptism, hospitality, Sabbath and so on – are the primary events and activities through which we encounter God and, as a result, our own transformation.

One such perspective is presented by Kenda Dean, who sees the role of practices in the context of young people's formation of identity. Dean views the time of adolescence as a period of life within which 'identities are works in progress' and that the task of adolescence itself is '[weaving] the shards of identity into something approaching an integrated whole'.[24] Dean proposes that youth ministry should include within its practice both a continuation of and corollaries of historic trajectories of Christian practice within which such faith identity is formed: solidarity experienced at Christian conferences and in small groups, worship that enables play, praise and lament, expressing practices of personhood such as chastity or hospitality, and the ability to experience union with Christ through the Eucharist.[25] Young people who participate in youth ministry have access to forms of practice that can transform

---

[23] Mark H. Senter, 'The Three-Legged Stool of Youth Ministry', in *Agenda for Youth Ministry: Cultural Themes in Faith and Church*, ed. Dean Borgman and Christine Cook (London: SPCK, 1998), 24–35 (28–9).

[24] Dean also takes this as a general view for all persons, just heightened in adolescence; Kenda Creasy Dean, *Practicing Passion: Youth and the Quest for a Passionate Church* (Grand Rapids, MI: Eerdmans, 2004), 24.

[25] See Dean, *Practicing Passion*, 155, for a summary of this 'constellation of contemporary practices'.

their identity. As Dean says, 'As we participate in practices of self-giving love [pathos], the holy spirit tenders a habitus of passionate responsiveness to God that becomes so ingrained in us that it defines us as Christians.'[26]

Presenting the pastoral relationship as central to the practice of youth ministry is perhaps a crucial dimension to the emergence of the full-time worker. Drawing on the pastoral theological texts that have inspired them, Dean and Foster argue that youth ministry is a task of *Godbearing*. The job of a pastor is as much to enable people to 'bring to life their understanding of faith' (to be midwives) as it is to provide solutions to problems or dilemmas (to be medics).[27]

Dorothy Bass sees that the key function of the youth worker, as pastor, is to be a 'tradition bearer', to introduce and involve young people in the historic practices of the Christian faith and to work with young people to enable them to reappraise and reappropriate such practices. The youth minister then becomes an advocate for such interpretations of 'tradition' within the broader community of faith, but also, importantly, acts to temper innovations by suggesting how these might in effect be 'unfaithful' to the community. Again, then, the role of the youth worker as pastoral agent is reasserted in the midst of highlighting how practices are inclusive of young people.[28]

Youth ministry in this approach is pastoral-mission practice that seeks to find and name the Christian practices through which young people can find transformed faith and identity. This has a resonance with the mission approach and in some ways reflects a greater emphasis on the theological understanding of youth ministry away from its roots in 'Christian education'. We are doing this because we have begun to recognize the need to engage actively in faith formation – that this involves not just socialization and education, but also transformation. This affirms what we carry in

---

[26] Dean, *Practicing Passion*, 159.
[27] Dean and Foster, *The Godbearing Life*.
[28] Dorothy C. Bass and Don C. Richter, *Way to Live: Christian Practices for Teens* (Nashville, TN: Upper Room Books, 2002).

our Christian tradition as of vital importance, but stresses that this needs to be more fully and intentionally conducted. As Mark Yaconelli identifies, we need to actively engage in practices that help us connect with the presence of God, and our contemplative traditions make space for this.[29] What this adds to the mix of youth ministry practices is the recognition that faith is formed through participation, particularly in the historic practices of the Christian faith but also in the ways in which these might be reconstituted or reinvented. Such practices then need to be considered as we think about the balance of enculturation and inculturation, and the way in which education seeks to enable 'critical awareness' of faith.

Taken together, these approaches offer a map of the types of activity that youth ministry engages in. This map can be envisaged as a set of connected practices that have their origins in each of the perspectives above (see Figure 1).

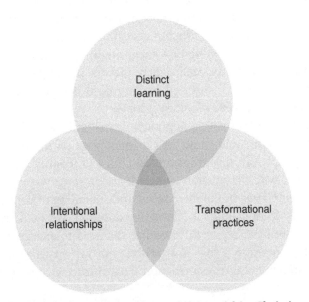

Figure 1 **Distinct but overlapping activities within Christian youth ministry**

---

[29] Mark Yaconelli, *Contemplative Youth Ministry* (London: SPCK, 2006), 5–6.

Some contexts for pastoral mission might privilege one or another of these spheres. In practice most youth ministry exists in the overlaps of these approaches, and distinctions are rapidly closing as the context for work with young people becomes reliant on the effective use of each of these methods. The challenge facing youth ministry now is how to evolve these practices to better address the challenge of faith formation in a secular age: that is, how to move on from seeing the problem as being about stemming institutional decline, towards better appreciating the shifting nature of belief, spirituality and faith as the conditions where faith generation is now required. It is through the deliberate merging of these approaches to form a general approach to faith generation that youth ministry can effectively build on the insights gained through practice over the past few decades. It is the appreciation of how this might be apparent in the actual practice of youth ministry, and how we can learn from this, that lies at the heart of the next sections looking at actual practice.

Forming youth ministries for faith generation: ideal types and actual practice

Youth ministry is a complex and sometimes contradictory response to young people's faith formation, but it is a response that has been evolving through the wisdom of actual practice. That we have 'youth ministry' highlights the fact that as a Church we have recognized the need for some clear interventions in our pastoral-mission work to facilitate young people's faith formation. This work has within it activity that promotes distinctive learning, is based on intentional relationships and seeks to enable participation in transformative practices. Each context where youth ministry occurs will be different. Some, as noted, will be directed towards young people in the Church and others outwards. The contexts I have highlighted are best approached in slightly different ways. In the coming chapters I will explore cases of actual practice to examine how the mix of activities observed in those groups contributes to faith formation – and the challenges of choice, sense and use.

In looking at actual practice I want to build on the general outline of youth work activities discussed in this chapter.

Growing faith: two contexts for investigating faith generation

The research I conducted involved two in-depth case studies of youth ministry, one based on the 'inside-out' model of a church-based youth group, and the other predicated on the 'outside-in' approach. I chose these two contexts on the basis that they were growing. In the case of the church-based group – which I call Impact – young people here had made clear decisions to remain in their church and to be Christian. In the mission drop-in project – which I call No. 1 – there was a mix of young people who were connected to the group, but a core who had become Christians through this connection. I gathered views from young people in individual and group interviews and spent time observing the activities they engaged in.

Impact is a youth group for 14–18-year-olds attached to a moderately sized Anglican church (175 adults on the electoral roll) in a residential area of a large city. The parish is a small geographical area and over 50 per cent of the church attendees do not live within the parish, a facet replicated in the group itself. Impact is the current 'incarnation' of the youth group at the church. The group under this name was started by the church's first salaried youth worker in 1993. However, the church has a heritage in youth work and there has been some form of identifiable and continuous youth provision since the 1950s.

The majority of young people are the teenage children of families from the church that hosts and runs Impact. Some young people who attend are from families who attend other churches and these young people often go to both the family church and the host church. A small minority in the group have no familial contact to church and have come along through friendships with members.

The young people in Impact are mainly 'middle class'. Parents are employed as professionals, teachers, or in responsibility-holding service sector positions. There is a range of family incomes, but most are able to afford the trips and weeks away that the group provides. Nearly all the group members appear to have enough financial resources to go regularly to concerts or the cinema, and most have items such as iPhones or similar devices. The group are all white British, apart from two members.

Impact is centred on a weekly meeting, with a set programme for each school term. A typical meeting involves social time at the start and planned activities around the theme of the night, some-times including a short talk as a prelude to group work and, on other occasions, no 'talk' but a variety of activities from which to choose. These activities might be a Bible study, group work around discussion points, reflective prayer activities, or artwork. In addi-tion most, but not all, meetings will have some form of worship, either within the main church area with a band comprising young people and leaders, or more reflective worship with music played through the sound system. Whatever the format, there is little sense of formality in these activities – there is a lot of 'banter' between leaders and the young people, though talks are usually listened to well. Engagement in activities varies. At times I noted young people to be highly active and participative, especially when themes involved cultural references or 'meaty debate' on topics such as other faiths or topics that impinge upon their feelings and ambitions, such as the nature of achievement. At times during some meetings, I noted that while issues under discussion were not focused on the activities, the group members did not show disengagement with the topic. Rather, young people were having their own conversations about the theme; at other times, though, they were just chatting about other issues and interests.

The session programme is defined, determined and delivered by the youth leaders. In meetings during which theme areas are chosen, a number of factors are considered. The first involves reflection on the previous term: what worked well or did not work well in terms of programmed input; what particular issues or positive experiences (of life in general or specifically connected to faith) were reported to the leaders by the young people in the group; which areas of 'Christian formation' are considered important or appropriate. The ideas generated from these discussions are then used to shape a programme for the term. Thus, when the young people come to Impact, the meeting theme, content and learning objectives as well as the worship, reflection and prayer activities have been predetermined and prepared by the youth leaders, and the meeting follows this running order.

Impact also has a set of small groups – two for boys and two for girls – set up for older and younger members of the youth group. These happen in either young people's homes, the church building or during social trips to local amenities. These were started as a result of conversations between leaders and young people, during which the young people reported that the main Impact session did not enable them to 'go deep enough' into issues and faith questions. These groups do not follow the main meeting programme but set their agenda week to week or month to month in response to the young people's expressed interests. The youth leader can then prepare the next couple of sessions. The groups for the older young people have focused on discussion about topical issues or Bible studies. They also have a more pastoral focus, allowing young people to discuss issues of concern and pray for one another.

In addition to the weekly meeting and small groups, there are occasional 'planned' social activities, such as bowling trips and a day trip to the beach, as well as weekends (or weeks) away as a group. Upcoming events are listed on the group's noticeboard in the church foyer, and pictures of previous events are in a gallery on the balcony. There is an annual trip to Spring Harvest, or 'Springy' as the young people call it. Beyond these organized activities, young people do meet up to hang out outside the group time and there are certain friendship groups for whom this is a regular occurrence. Some of the young people also see one another at church services. Very few of the young people go to the same school, making Impact meetings and activities a primary social context for their friendships. Some of the friendship groups of young people are based on their family's connections as longstanding members of their churches. They are not just members of the same youth group but friends who have grown up and gone on holiday together. The current cohort of church young people have grown up knowing that the Impact group is part of the 'scene', and many of them have had older siblings who have been members. There is anticipation, excitement and expectation generated by 'graduating' into this older group.

Impact generates the impression that it provides a 'home' for young people within the church community. Impact has a distinct identity evidenced by the enthusiasm to join and the way in which this group name is used with familiarity. However, it also has a visible presence within the wider church, with a crossover time between the end of an evening service and the start of the group, as well as its 'own' area on a balcony within the main church building. This area is decorated with artwork done by the young people, both from several years ago and more recently, as well as photographs from previous events or trips. As I will discuss more in a moment, the young people think of Impact as their 'home in church' – where church is 'for them'.

No. 1 is based in a converted terraced house in a large town, and is run by a local Christian youth organization. No. 1 is an 'outreach' centre in two senses of the term. First, it employs youth workers engaged in youth work based on an outreach model – going into the local area to make contact with young people to raise the profile of the 'drop-in' and its activities. It has also been set up to be distinctly 'outreach' in a missional sense, since the purpose of the drop-in is to provide not only a place for young people to go after school but also a space and platform for engaging young people in conversation about faith.

As a drop-in, No. 1 has a fluid attendance. According to one of the senior workers, the total number of different young people who come into the drop-in is around 80. Of these, there is a core of 20 who attend a couple of times a week. Since opening, a group of around ten young people have become Christians, primarily through their involvement in the drop-in. In this time, No. 1 has also relaxed its initial stance of discouraging young people who already class themselves as Christian from coming. This means that there is also a group of young people active in local churches now connected to the drop-in, mostly as volunteers.

The young people who come to the drop-in live in the imme-diate locality and reflect the social background of the area – pre-dominantly working class. Some of the young people are from what are considered economically disadvantaged backgrounds and this has enabled the drop-in to gain some grant funding for equip-ment. A small number of the kids go to a local grammar school, but most go to the large comprehensive school in the area. The members of the youth work team from No. 1 are also active in these schools, running lunchtime clubs and taking RE lessons.

No. 1 was started in order to engage with young people who had no previous contact with the Church. Their families are not churchgoers and, at least until coming into contact with No. 1, neither were any of their peers. Furthermore, some of the young people for whom involvement in No. 1 has been formative in terms of faith have developed strong connections to youth groups in local churches, particularly one group (named Crucial) attached to a local Anglican church.

No. 1 is open most weekdays in the year: its main opening times are after school. These times vary in school holidays, and special activities are put on within these periods. The drop-in has a 'homely' feel; it is, after all, in a converted terrace house in a residential street. There are soft furnishings, tables and chairs. Anyone who comes in through the door is offered tea, coffee or a cold drink by one of the youth leaders. The team is made up of paid members of staff, young adults on a 'gap year' programme and local volunteers (full time and part time). Since the staff and gap-year team also work in the local schools they know a good percentage of young people from this context as well as from the drop-in.

There are a number of resources for young people and leaders to use to interact with one another, such as card games and board games, a PlayStation, craft activities and a music system. Upstairs, young people can use the computer network to access the internet (usage is monitored as part of a grant requirement) and they are allowed into a room that serves as an office for the youth workers. The drop-in is also, then, the home base of the organization; it is the central point from which it is administered and often the location for meetings and small groups. Some of the workers remain in the office while the drop-in is in operation. However, young people are very comfortable walking in and chatting in this space.

A drop-in session is exactly that – young people drop in to No. 1 at any point within the session. On some days individuals stay for the whole time, while on other occasions they might only come in for a few minutes. On some weeks there are planned activities that the youth workers have scheduled. On other weeks leaders are simply encouraged to seek to focus conversations on particular issues or around faith. These conversations provide a focal point for activities or contribute to a learning agenda that the youth workers have identified and chosen in response to specific incidents or reflections. Such reflections and actions occur on a day-by-day and longer-term basis. In addition, before and after each session the leaders meet to discuss and pray about the session and issues of concern or interest with young people with whom they have talked.

The drop-in is a 'local' – its feel is like that of a local café or local pub! Conversation often flows around local issues: supporting the football club, talking about mutual friends or school life and news, and other aspects of social life. No. 1 does not have a programme and pattern of meetings but it is run as intentional youth work. The workers are influential in setting the 'tone' and sometimes the 'theme' of conversation in particular sessions. In addition to the after-school session, the drop-in is used in the evening for thematic activities. In the past these have included a young men's group, an Alpha course and video nights. These activities, along with trips to summer camps and Christian festivals, have also instigated a commitment to support young people in their 'discipleship'. This includes meeting with a one-to-one mentor during drop-in time.

The Christian aspect of this youth work provision is not in any way hidden from the young people (or families when contact is required or generated). Over the entrance and front window of the drop-in there is a large sign that refers to the organization as identifiably Christian. Young people often refer to No. 1 as 'the

Christian place'. This of course does not demonstrate that the young people know what the Christian ethos and missional basis for work means. It does indicate, however, that the faith aspect of the work is not being hidden; indeed the opposite is the case. Young people get to know this quickly, though, as the decor and activities make the Christian ethos of No. 1 very obvious.

In some of these sessions there was a notable resistance to having to 'sit and listen' to the question-time sessions. However, conversation within everyday drop-in sessions provides the primary opportunity for exchange of views on faith, and the youth workers are very proactive in seeking young people's opinions. There is a general ethos of participation; there is a suggestion box and a graffiti wall, and the young people, who perceive these to be a genuine way of 'being listened to', use them. The enthusiasm young people at No. 1 have for the place and resources within it illustrates that they enjoy and appreciate this provision, just as their relaxed manner with the leaders suggests value for their support and interest in them.

The focus of the next three chapters is to explore how young people view participation in these youth ministry projects in relation to the task of trying to be Christian.[30]

Questions for discussion

1 Think about the youth ministry context with which you are familiar. What function does it play in the life of your church beyond just providing activities for young people?
2 If you are a youth worker or leader, analyse your own activities over the past six months and identify which of the elements of distinctive learning, intentional relationships and transformative practices are present in your work. How do you understand their roles?

---

[30] The quotations in the coming chapters are taken from interviews with young people (aged 14–18) and youth workers and leaders gathered over a two-year period as part of a doctorate investigating the influence of youth ministry on young people's faith. I concluded this research in 2010 and revisited the data for this book in the light of findings of the *From Anecdote to Evidence* report. The names given are pseudonyms.

3 If you can, why not write out a portrait of practice similar to that written here for Impact and No. 1.

4 Think about your own story of owning your own faith and reflect on what you gained through participation in youth ministry, or talk to a young person you know about what he or she feels are the most important aspects of this ministry.

3

Making implausible choices: youth groups and faith identity

————◆————

Look for somewhere that you can talk to people about it.
So, look for something like Impact or No. 1 ... Look for
something like that in your local area, go into the church
and say ... 'cos that will help you more than anything you
could know. (Marcus)

The first challenge of faith generation is choice. In this chapter I
will begin to unpack what young people say about their experience
of choosing to believe and how youth ministry helps to make faith
a 'plausible choice'.

Young people's experience of faith is varied. However, taking
note of some actual experience can help to paint a picture of
what choosing to believe looks and feels like for young people –
how they experience the pressure of choice on faith in a secular
age. The pressures for young people who have been 'brought up
to believe' appear to be different from the pressures experienced
by those 'brought into faith'. For both groups of young people
there is, however, a deep sense of choice to believe as a fundamental issue of identity. The experience of choice is not one
of having open options, but one of opting to be open about
the positive and negative impact of believing. Young people
show sophistication in their appreciation of this requirement
for faith in a secular age. They also offer a clear understanding
of the importance of the places that help in this task – the
location and group within which the choice to believe becomes
possible.

Choice: making faith personal

The idea that faith is a choice seems obvious. As we explored earlier, the need to 'own' faith is the core of Westerhoff's faith development theory – choosing a faith of his or her own is an essential aspect of how a young person's faith develops. Holding faith in a secular age requires a choice, whether one has been raised in a Christian context or is encountering Christian belief for the first time. Affirming the need for a personal faith has been a core aspect of educational, missional and formational approaches to youth ministry. This has been particularly the case within evangelical Protestant contexts. However, the need for such a choice is a deeper societal factor that goes beyond a particular understanding of conversion. Faith commitment in a secular age is not an issue of rational consideration of belief. It is a choice around identity.

To suggest that choice is the first key challenge of faith generation also seems obvious. Yet the requirement of having to 'choose' to believe is, in regard to Christian faith, a relatively new phenomenon, as Duncan MacLaren discusses in his book *Mission Implausible*. MacLaren argues that in previous times in our Christian era the ability to choose to believe was not an option. Rather, being Christian provided for a 'general need for identity within a sacred society'.[1] However, in a secular age such a choice is not only available, but has increasingly become difficult to make and keep. This is not to suggest that religion in previous times was without dissent or difference – far from it. What it does imply, though, is that for faith to be held today a person *needs* to make an active decision to make 'faith' a part of his or her life and to make being a person of faith part of his or her self-understanding.

Close listening to young people's experiences reveals this relationship between choice and identity. It is the requirement to make such a choice that is the first defining aspect of the proximal impact of secularization.

---

[1] Duncan MacLaren, *Mission Implausible: Restoring Credibility to the Church*, Studies in Religion and Culture (Milton Keynes: Paternoster Press, 2004), 101.

Brought up to believe: faith, choice and identity

Young people raised in Christian families have a strong recognition that being Christian is something 'they are'; Christianity is not just something they believe. Phillip – a young man whose family is well integrated into a church – captures this sentiment eloquently. When asked what being a Christian means to him he says:

> Imagining my life without Christianity would just be . . . really odd, because all my friends and everything I've experienced in Christianity has become my life . . . I wouldn't have my closest friends, my family; everything would just fall to pieces, I think. It's what holds together my life. Without it, I would feel really weird . . . completely.

Belief in God is important to Phillip and he sees faith in these terms as well, but there is something important in how he and other young people capture faith as identity – as a part of who they are, not what they believe. This depth of faith identity is accompanied, however, by vulnerability when it comes to establishing their own identity as Christian young adults. Their families and church communities have in this context been very effective at inspiring faith. They have been brought up to believe. As Marcus, another young person in this group (Impact), explains in his reflection on growing up in a Christian home:

> Well, I think that because it's the way I was brought up, and that sort of thing, the values of Christianity, in itself, are ingrained in my person.

There are questions here about how the family and the Church help to establish this sense of ingrained identity in childhood. Hattie, one of the young people in Impact without a church background, expressed the impression that others in Impact are 'all Christians from, like, the very beginning'. She finds it a challenge in this group to work out her beliefs and feels that all the other young people appear to know how 'to think like Christians'. Given the boundaries of what I am looking into here, this needs to be affirmed as a crucial place to begin in faith generation, which I will return to later. What is interesting for faith generation is that given this robust formation in childhood, one might expect in a group like this that growing in faith is a matter of development, not choice. This does not appear to be the case, however, as such an upbringing is both a gift and a predicament when young people move into a phase of life where their own choice to believe takes precedence over family faith.

Hattie, for instance, indicates in a written account of her Faith Story[2] that she 'never really understood about God' and Christianity until she started going to camps and conferences with the group. She grew up in a Christian family, where there was a clear focus on family participation in church, prayer and faith practices in the home. Phillip, who as indicated above expresses a deep sense of faith being entwined in his identity, also talks about having to undergo the process of owning faith:

> It wasn't sort of like a pinnacle moment, where I sort of thought, 'Yeah, this is actually true.' It was sort of little things at a time, that gradually progressed into my own faith rather than living off my parents'.

There is a lot of 'work' involved in this process. Amelia talks of a similar development of her own faith identity but is more emphatic about it being her own sense of independent choice; about her choice to be baptized, she said, 'This was a decision I made on my own, without any pressure from my parents/friends.' It is unlikely that such a 'free choice' can really be claimed. Her family and faith community would continue to influence and encourage this choice. What is important here is that being able to establish choice as *mine* is vital. It is vital in that it marks a move from 'ascribed' to 'attained' identity – that being Christian is not something you are born into, but something you choose to be.

There is, though, a certain contingency about faith being a personal choice. Marcus, with his ingrained sense of faith, talks

---

[2] I asked young people involved in my research to write a short account of their experience of being a Christian and to outline the key events and experiences in their 'Faith Story'.

about choosing personal faith after 'experiencing' God at a local youth worship event. Yet in interview he gives a hint of doubt about this being a personal choice:

> I chose to believe in the fact that Christ died and came back to life to save the world from sin; that was my own choice, I think . . . [My parents] brought me up with these values, and they've kind of let me know exactly what they believe, and I've made the choice myself to believe the same things . . . to some extent.

This indicates that faith identity requires some supportive confidence around this decision – a confidence that comes from within in Amelia's experience or from elsewhere for some others. For these young people an ingrained sense of faith is not enough; it needs to become personal. Alone, this is not a surprising feature of their development of personal identity. A personal faith identity is not a theory for these young people; it is *their* sense of self and self-esteem that is at stake. In response to a suggestion from another young person that 'being a Christian was like being given someone else's clothes and being told you've got to wear this, this is yours now', Gerard ventured:

> I think it's more about being comfortable . . . being comfortable wearing those clothes, like – instead of wearing it, sort of, ashamed, like, in your room, like, taking it off before you go – you just don't care, and you go out wearing it, like . . . confidence in . . . what beliefs you hold . . . being comfortable with how people view you.

For young people brought up to believe, the challenge of choosing a personal faith involves negotiating the depth to which being a Christian is ingrained into their sense of identity, being able to own this as they develop a more independent sense of self, and holding and expressing this aspect of 'who they are' in environments away from the church.[3] What, then, is the situation for young people who have not grown up in such contexts?

---

[3] For a more detailed examination of this process see Malan Nel, 'Identity Formation and the Challenge of Individuation in Youth Ministry', *Journal of Youth Ministry* 1, no. 2 (Spring 2003): 79–102.

Brought into belief: faith identity as choice

The experiences of young people from the No. 1 project are different from those in the youth group Impact and, as might be expected, they do not have the same sense of faith being 'ingrained' into their sense of self as the young people in Impact. Yet, forming a sense of identity that incorporates their faith is a task that the young people at No. 1 appear to be engaged in, and the role of the group is vital in this. This involves faith being a choice that connects with the identity issues particular young people have.

Bryony, for example, recounts in her Faith Story how participation in No. 1 began to enable her to rethink and re-evaluate some of the negative ways in which she regarded herself:

> Well, things got really bad at home and something that I'm not really proud of started to happen, I started to use my body (*sic*). I would cut myself and drink a lot, too much that would make me be sick because my body wasn't mature enough to handle it. I would keep doing this maybe once, twice a week.

The workers in No. 1 did seek to address these issues in supportive conversation and through this to work with Bryony to help her consider additional advice or support. In addition, though, Bryony makes connections to how her own emerging faith has begun to have an influence on the way she sees herself. A provocation Bryony attaches to this was attending a dedication service for the baby of Martin and Jane, two of the leaders.

> I finally stop this after [Jane's baby's] dedication when I realized that well I was being stupid or . . . that day at the service was great, loads of people were there to bring him into the church, everyone was so happy and I just thought that I would love this to be me, but then I look at all the bad things I have done and I start to think, why would this God want me? I decided that day to change my ways, going to do all these things that use my body, and well try to set a good example for their young people coming to No. 1. I have also tried to learn more about God.

For Bryony, participation in No. 1 is part of the emerging of faith identity. Jane had also had an earlier miscarriage that many of the young people were aware of. It was also a topic that Jane reports she discussed with Bryony, especially the sense of how faith was possible in the face of such a trauma.

Sarah's Faith Story is similar to Bryony's. Her mum left home when Sarah was 14 and she has had a string of illnesses for which she has been hospitalized. From spending time with her it was clear to me that the love and friendship she has found at No. 1 are pivotal in her choice to become a Christian:

> I believe in God because he has helped me out big time and he has never left me and has never let me down. I became a Christian because my life was crap, I had to put up with a lot of things. I couldn't cope with that, my mum and dad breaking up and my sister going into prison . . . and I wanted the pain to go away.

This depth of impact at a personal level is important in helping us to see why faith becomes a choice these young people consider. It of course raises clear ethical considerations for Christian youth work – in how one works appropriately with such young people and how exploring faith is a part of this. However, even where a young person does not openly present or discuss such issues, the depth at which faith and identity are connected is illustrated by Mark's story.

Mark came to faith through attending an Alpha course run through the drop-in. It was, though, the transformation in his sense of self that he was keen to emphasize in his Faith Story. I asked him what difference being a Christian has made to him. He replied:

> It changes the way I think about myself a lot different, because I never used to think about myself as anything . . . it gives me self-esteem and it gives me partial confidence, 'cos I'm not very confident, anyway. And it just lets me express who I am.

For the young people who have 'dropped in' to faith this choice is deeply connected to their sense of self. These young people do not have the same types of doubts that the young people raised as Christians do, but they too talk about becoming Christian in relation to how this connects to their identity. As I will discuss later, how faith makes sense is also an important aspect of a choice to believe, but this too cannot be taken in isolation from the way faith and identity are closely intertwined.

Continual choice: managing personal faith

Young people experience the choice to believe at the level of identity. While the substance of faith remains important, this understanding is helpful in beginning to see how the proximal impact of secularization is felt in real life. Yet choice is not a one-off experience. Holding faith in a secular age requires young people to choose continually. This is not a matter of 'keeping options open' – though for some young people that might be the case; rather, continual choice here is experienced as a requirement of believing. As with choosing a personal faith, this too is experienced in different ways by young people who have been brought up to believe and by those who have come to faith as teenagers.

This continual choosing is required because in a secular age religious beliefs and practices are not only open to question, they are at risk of losing both the meanings and security they might once have conveyed. Even where family and community have deeply embedded values and practices, choosing to continue to belong and believe is an active process because such values and views are not upheld elsewhere. MacLaren, as a sociologist, discusses this in terms of *plausibility*: the ability for a person to believe and express his or her faith is at risk because the social context in which this is held comes under threat. What is pertinent for faith generation is that MacLaren sees the point at which this happens as being at the juncture of young adulthood: particularly for young people raised in contexts where faith is 'natural' or 'normal', there comes an inevitable point where a choice to continue to believe is 'forced upon young people'.[4] What is more, a choice to believe

---

[4] MacLaren, *Mission Implausible*, 101.

is complicated because people experience a variety of places as 'plausibility shelters', which requires constant management. As MacLaren identifies, 'contemporary people inhabit a bewildering multiplicity of [places of plausibility] – what seems plausible in the family, the workplace, or in the mass media, may vary widely between one context and another.'[5]

This reality leads to a constant sense of self-checking, in the presentation of self in different social contexts, of working out the right things to say and do. It is also, perhaps, empowering – we have the freedom to choose to be very different in very different contexts. Listening to young people shows us that for them faith is similarly held in tension between these places of plausibility. Our choices define us.

Faith on a safety catch: choice under challenge

Listening to young people who have been raised as Christians talk about their experience of living out their faith gives the impression that this resembles traversing two different worlds: one where faith is plausible and possible, and one where it is less plausible and harder to hold. When they are asked to describe the high and low points of faith there is frequent linking of high points to the experience of God in worship, with school viewed as a low point. Gerard came up with a term for describing the reality of traversing these two worlds – he called it 'faith on a safety catch'. Gerard had reflected that being a Christian in school was for him a 'horrible' experience. His tactic for coping with this was to wait it out until the weekend when he got to be with his youth group. Gerard here identifies something important about faith in a secular age that contributes to the proximal impact of secularization:

> You're completely different around school friends, because I get into that school mode where I'm one of the only people who's actually a Christian and flaunts it and says, 'I'm a Christian, I don't really care.' . . . When I get into weekends, there are other people around me who are Christians and I don't have

---

[5] MacLaren, *Mission Implausible*, 111.

that safety 'on' any more. Because, at school, I kind of put on
like a safety catch . . . 'cos you're put into a mode where you
are on guard, in a way, at school.

This experience of crossing between these two worlds is not simple
and involves a continual management of the choice to believe.
Gerard is not suggesting that he hides his Christian identity in
school; he flaunts it, but being in the school environment requires
him to be alert (safety on) to how he represents himself and
how he is being perceived. Gerard is describing choice as active
and ongoing, a constant 'issue' that has to be managed. Having
identified the theme of 'safety catch theory', he uses it to try to
explain this:

[My safety catch] is a mode where I'm just trying to stay focused
and I try not to let anyone let me come away from my faith. I try
not to let anyone persuade me that I'm actually wrong, because
I know that it could happen.

This is Gerard's tactic for 'coping' with the challenge of enacting
or representing himself as a Christian. Susanna, Jessica and Frankie
discussed a similar dilemma around 'being the same person' in
school and in their group. They discussed how much easier it was
to be 'kinder' in the group and how they wanted to be more like
this in other contexts. In this way, the group acts not just as a
place where they find it easier to reflect the values they aspire to,
but also as the place where such values are nurtured and encouraged. As Frankie makes clear:

I think it's the whole idea about being surrounded by others
who perhaps help you or comfort you . . . whereas if you're going
through struggles and you're surrounded by non-Christians and
a non-Christian way of living, it's harder to kind of pick yourself
back up.

However, Simon says that while he finds it hard to tell people he's
a Christian, he finds that it helps when people criticize him because
then he has to 'actually think about things, and I think that sort
of strengthens my faith'. For Simon, defending his faith at school

becomes a source of strength in underscoring his own sense of faith identity, not in any sense to try to convert or persuade others, but as an act of securing his own sense of identity through representing himself and his views. This is captured in the way in which young people discuss the importance of 'outing themselves' as Christian. As Phillip says:

> I would say if the chance came up for you to admit your Christianity, no matter how hard it is, seriously try to admit that you are a Christian, because you'll feel a lot better, I'm sure. And even if you do get teased a little bit or – you'll get rewarded for it in the end.

The 'reward' to which Phillip refers is not 'spiritual' (though this might be being implied) but rather a tangible sense of self-confidence: 'You'll end up feeling a lot better . . . you'll just feel better if you admit you're a Christian,' he goes on to say. This sense of a defended identity means that every occasion on which the boundaries are crossed between the places where faith is perceived as a struggle, and where faith is perceived as strength, requires some sort of processing by young people. This experience is similar for young people who have become Christians. Here, though, in addition to the school environment the family and home can also contribute to this negative pressure.

Faith under suspicion: challenging choices

A significant issue for young people in No. 1 is the apathy or open hostility shown by parents and friends to their becoming Christians. Mark says that when he told his family he'd become a Christian, 'my dad called God a really horrible name', and his father continues to 'wind me up and . . . say horrible things'. In response to this Mark says that he copes with this by choosing to

> ignore him, and that. I pray to God to help me to ignore him. My mum, she's not Christian, but she knows there's a God, she believes there's a God, so she'll help me if I need any help. But, basically, it's all here at No. 1 that help me the most, definitely, yeah.

Prayer and coming to No. 1 are given weight in being able to cope with the difficulties Mark faces. I asked him to expand on this.

> I usually come up [to No. 1] when I can, and that helps me keep in touch with [God], because I'm around people who believe in God . . . without this I would just lose faith.

Here, then, the connection to the group is vital in coping with this negative pressure on Mark's choice to believe. Others show this too. Nicky expresses similar sentiments to Gerard: experiences away from the group provoke the need to strengthen faith by being in a place where 'believing' is valued.

> If I didn't go here [No. 1], I think I would have lost my faith a bit, and because, like, there's no one in my family that is Christian. My mum, she's not Christian, but she believes there's a God, and, yet, sometimes, I kind of like say, 'But why does this happen? Why does this happen?' I don't know. But, if I hadn't come here, they would have been saying these things, and I would have thought, 'Hmm, that's true, so I won't believe in that.'

The challenge of holding a faith identity in school is perceived as being a struggle and was a chief aspect of the support gained from participating in the group. Young people in No. 1 encounter antagonistic feelings and provocative questions but in general adopt a more robust stance. The young people in No. 1 display their faith identity quite overtly. Monica talked about a time when she took her Bible into school (so she could have it for the drop-in after school). When a friend at school challenged her on why she had a Bible, she replied, "Cos I'm a Christian", and then loudly repeated this to everybody in the room. Abigail talked with pride about the conversations provoked by her wearing a 'hoodie' with 'APG' on it (mimicking the GAP logo), which stands for 'Always Praising God'. This willingness to be seen and identified as Christians suggests that school might not be such a negative environment for faith. I asked her if her friends who weren't Christians were bothered by her 'conversion':

> They didn't care . . . most of them came here [to No. 1], anyway,
> so that was all cool. There used to be a divide in, like, RE class,
> and you had the Christians one side and the non-Christians the
> other, and we'd just, like, be saying stuff, and the others would
> just be shouting at us. But, most people took it OK.

This overt 'performance' belies the fact that these young Christians
also recognize some subtleties are required in representing themselves as 'Christian', especially in interactions with non-Christian
friends. Here Monica talks about a particular understanding she
has of the dynamics of relating faith to her school friends:

> When I'm talking to my friends about, like, being a Christian
> and everything, and they've got problems and I'm chatting to
> them . . . I'd say to them, 'Well, I'm going to go all Christian on
> you now, so, if you just listen, you don't have to agree with me,
> I'm not going to try and convert you, I'm just going to say
> something', and they'll sit and listen to me and everything.

Monica talks about 'going all Christian' as a tactic to put others
at ease about her faith. By distancing herself like this, she can play
a role and be comfortable in talking about God and offering to
pray for people. Together with the experiences of negotiating the
challenge of a family environment where a choice to believe is
met with hostility or criticism, young people who have chosen
faith also face the pressure of having to perform the identity they
have chosen. As with the young people brought up to believe,
they identify the group that helps to nurture their faith as vital in
helping them to achieve this. It is this role of the youth group
in enabling choice that I turn to next.

Choice places: making faith plausible

The plausibility of faith in a secular age is complex. In sociological
terms the plausibility of faith requires concrete social structures –
family, school and church – to provide communities within which
the credibility and cohesion of beliefs can be established. These
are often accurately cast as the solid walls where belief can be

assured. In this analysis religious belief is often viewed critically as occurring in the tight social structures of 'closed' religious groups, leading to the dogmatic faith of fundamentalism. More subtly, as Pete Ward has shown, this social structure can be seen more benignly as a 'subculture' that has its own patterns and practices, values and symbols. In this vein being Christian is just your 'thing', like being into country music or *Star Trek*. What is very important for our discussion is that some form of clear social dimension to a life of faith is vital for faith generation. Westerhoff envisioned an ecology of social institutions that helped to secure and support faith development. Addressing the issue of plausibility highlights the fact that this is no longer the case. For faith to be plausible we have to rebuild this ecology.

It is helpful here to draw a little deeper into understanding the plausibility of faith. Doing so does not undermine the belief that faith is inspired by God through his Spirit; it simply affirms that having faith is not an individual pursuit. Being Christian, being the Church, has a distinct social dimension, which is an expression partly of our faith and partly of the community within which faith is formed. Plausibility theory states that all faith groups need legitimizing practices and even ones that strike a more open chord – such as apologetics – that function to help provide coherence to beliefs. Such practices not only require solid social structures, but also draw on wider 'virtual structures' of memory, identity and imagination. Here symbols, language and shared meanings in conversation within communities of faith are particularly important. Drawing again on the work of Duncan MacLaren, what is distinct for faith in a secular age is that there is precariousness to these structures. In most churches today such conversations are limited to 'small Bible study groups, chance meetings with other Christians in the supermarket and [through] the shelves of Christian bookshops'.[6] To counter this, MacLaren argues that we need to build *plausibility shelters* – places where faith is made 'possible'. Such places are increasingly important because we live in a society where alternative plausibility structures are available

---

[6] MacLaren, *Mission Implausible*, 101.

and will inevitably encroach upon or clash with that of the faith communities in which children are raised.

The discussion of the experiences of young people in this chapter earths this theory in their actual experience of being Christian. It begins to sketch out how youth groups are an important aspect of such plausibility shelters; indeed young people perceive them as crucial in the formation and support of faith. This is not to reduce faith to merely this social reinforcement alone, but attention to the places where young people can be Christian is a vital element of faith generation. It is clear that such places need to be built as part of this task.

A place to be Christian: making plausible choices

As previously discussed, supporting a plausible faith requires a community that can enable choice, sense and use. The core practices of Impact are all geared to respond to these needs. Choice, as discussed above, is gradual and ongoing. Here historic Christian practices such as testimony and baptism mix with more fluid lifestyle practices of youth culture to create robust places of plausible faith.

The Christian youth group – at least as exemplified by Impact – is intentionally structured around 'moving' young people through personal commitment marked by confirmation or baptism. Getting confirmed or baptized is a community rite of passage, but it is prompted and guided through involvement in Impact and associated activities. Amelia described in interview how she 'got really close to God over Spring Harvest . . . and I wanted to continue that closeness' and so she asked to be baptized. Amelia attends Impact as well as her Baptist church so baptism as a public confession of faith fits within her tradition. The Anglican young people in Impact do, though, show a similar approach to confirmation. As Amanda says:

My family and I have always been involved in church so I've always considered myself a Christian. When I was 15 I finally felt as though I really knew and loved God myself so I got confirmed.

The important link here to personal faith is that confirmation for Amanda is an active choice which centres on her own personal story rather than simply following a traditional rite of passage in teenage years. Perhaps it is like the experience of Michael, who said in his Faith Story that he had always thought of himself as a Christian, but got confirmed because he felt it was 'the right thing to do'. For these young Anglicans, confirmation is a little more of an ambivalent 'rite of passage', yet preparing for and being confirmed is a key pattern of practice in Impact; there is an annual area confirmation service and young people from Impact are encouraged to think about getting baptized or confirmed as soon as they join the group.

As we have seen, participation in their youth group is identified as highly significant for the young people who have been brought up to believe. This youth group is the place and community where they find the ability to discuss and reflect on their personal experience of faith. This participation is deeper, though, in that it also structures the way in which young people, over time, develop patterns and habits that support their faith. Phillip sheds some light on this when discussing how being in the group is helpful to him in combating doubts and difficulties:

> [Impact has] always been useful for me, when I've had problems or doubts and things, because *it's sort of become a ritual in my life*, with every Sunday, coming here, so it's always helped me when I've had doubts and stuff.

Given that he had just commented earlier that his initial desire in wanting to come to Impact was because 'all the older cool people had been there', I thought this change in attitude to be significant and wondered if 'ritual' was a positive thing for him. He reflected a little and said that coming to Impact

> sort of keeps some structure, because there's never, sort of, time for me to go off track, sort of thing, and do things that other people do at school, and stuff, because I have sort of set routines at weekends, which helps me, I think.

This aspect of the structure that coming to Impact provides for young people is seen in a discussion about the highs and lows of faith in one of the earlier focus groups. The conversation, noted earlier, about how difficult it was to be a Christian in school prompted Marcus to comment that:

> Yeah, it sounds a cliché but my whole week feels like a wait for the weekend, because you . . . I've got some fantastic friends at school, but still, then, there's still this hunger for God, sort of thing. It's like it's not like waiting for Saturday to go and hang out and have fun with your mates, it's like waiting for Sunday to go and see your mates who are Christians.

Here faith is seen as connected to the social context of gathering *as Christians* and this gathering is tied to a hunger for God. Impact is the place in which or through which the young people parti-cipate in practices where they experience God, and it is a place where their experience of community brings confidence and security. It is also a place where they are guided and encouraged to develop their own Faith Story, and where they can engage in questioning and learning about faith. It is also a place where they feel a sense of belonging as Christians, a sense of their com-munity, and a ritual and rhythm in their lives. In the final section of this data from Impact I will review what the leaders have to say on issues related to the data discussed so far.

The friendship base in Impact has a significance in 'holding people' in times when life (or faith) seems tricky and conferring a particular confidence about being a Christian. Gerard reports that during a time when his girlfriend was seriously ill, coming to Impact was what prevented him from 'jacking his faith in'. For Gerard it wasn't talking about these things so much as 'just com-ing' and being provoked by this to think, 'If there are great people like this then somebody must create them.' His reflection on this was not just that if he stopped coming he would miss his friends, but also that he would 'lose faith'. A comment from Jessica sum-marizes these sentiments well:

> Impact . . . it brings it all together and it makes it more real and it makes it more, kind of, there is, kind of, a group in the church that are . . . it links in with the whole friendship thing . . . there is a community like you in this church, whereas – I mean, it's

good that, you know, the whole church can be a community,
but a community that you fit in better.

Jessica talks later in this focus group about how this sense of community provides a platform for her own confidence. The benefit
of belonging is transferred to other areas of her life:

> You're so comfortable and you're so confident in Impact [it
> gives me a] non-caring attitude to just go out and think, kind
> of, 'If people don't accept me as who I am, then, you know,
> that's their problem, not mine.'

Impact, then, is a place to be Christian, a place that puts the choice
to believe at the heart of its purpose and provides a group culture
that supports this task. What, then, of the experience of young
people who have dropped in to faith?

A Christian place: making choice plausible

A similar appreciation is seen from young people who have come
into faith; they too need a place to be Christian, though their
journey to that point is different.

Initial motivations for coming to the drop-in vary. Some come
because school friends do, others because they are invited by
the workers, and a few because there is 'nothing else to do'. The
leaders of No. 1 do not try to hide the Christian nature of their
organization. The sign over the entrance and the work they undertake in schools clearly identifies them as a Christian group. Young
people who come into No. 1 know of it as a 'Christian place' and
this connotation is not entirely positive. In talking about their
first experiences of coming into No. 1, Abigail, Sarah and Bryony
clearly indicate this view of the centre:

> SARAH   I was bricking it. I thought it was going to be really
> divi [uncool, stupid].
> ABIGAIL   So did I! It's like, it's 'the Christian place' tonight –
> SARAH   Yeah, I thought it was going to be really divi.

Bryony suggests a degree of fear about coming into No. 1 as a
Christian place. Abigail writes in her Faith Story that she walked

up and down past the drop-in on three occasions before she 'picked up the courage' to come in. This may be an indication of the 'nerve' required to come to any new place. However, the indication in the data is that this is in part because of the connotations of No. 1 being a Christian place. Coming into the drop-in, then, is a significant act for these young people.

When they do come in, the experience reported is one of welcome and quickly finding out that this is a place that they want to come back to. At the same time, this experience confronts some of the stereotypes and anxieties about the Christian nature of No. 1. Abigail says:

> I couldn't believe the leaders were Christians. They weren't like your stereotypical Christians, like I thought from going to Rock Solid [an activity-based Christian youth event] a few years back.

In an interview she expanded on this a little:

> It was cool, because everyone was like, loving, you enjoyed yourself. It was a bit scary and, like, I quite liked talking to Gareth . . . one of the leaders that was here, he was cool, and Jane.

The experience of welcome should perhaps not be under-appreciated. From my observations the majority of young people appreciate and enjoy what the drop-in provides as a social space – the music, the warmth (especially on cold days) and the internet! Some of the young people have no objection to discussing their own understanding of faith. Some make their disinterest explicitly known, but keep coming back to the drop-in on a regular basis. Two observations are striking in underscoring the hospitable community of No. 1.

On one occasion a girl came into the drop-in and Martin, the senior worker, asked her how her drama performance had gone the previous day. She 'lit up' and went on to talk at length about how well it had gone. On another occasion a boy had cut his hand on some glass in a nearby road and his friends had brought him to the drop-in to get it looked at. This boy hadn't personally been before; his friends had and seemed to know that coming there meant his cut could be cleaned up. No. 1, then, has earned a space within the social world of these young people. While it maintains a distinct Christian identity, it also serves as an open and hospitable place where young people feel able to come and go – and where it is known that they can find certain forms of assistance. As well as being welcoming, No. 1 is also well run as a 'youth club'.

Within No. 1 there are also boundaries and codes for behaving that are not dissimilar to those in other youth work establishments. The rules and behaviour code in No. 1, though, do not merely convey the standards expected of participants, or even set boundaries for language. What is also encouraged in No. 1 is to 'display empathy' towards others. Young people come to adopt certain standards and behaviours that begin to influence the way they relate to one another and come to view themselves. Leaders focus on and work to achieve this culture and it is often discussed in the leaders' meetings before the drop-in opens.

I have already noted that for young people who have found faith through No. 1, continuing to come is seen as a pattern of their faith – shown by phrases such as 'coming here reminds me of what I believe'. Nicky puts it almost in a desperate sense:

> But I need something to lock me in, lock in, don't let me go . . . No. 1, and the leaders here, to lock me in, and to help me read the Bible.

This type of sentiment about participation as assuring a sense of self as Christian is different from that expressed by the young people in Impact. It is, though, evidence of a similar significance in how participation in No. 1 gives structure for a life of faith for these young people. Coming here is needed for them to hold faith. This centre is, for these young people, not only helping to form personal faith, but is also crucial in continuing to sustain this faith.

This leaves the Church with two competing challenges. First, to adapt our social structures and practices to provide the robust types of 'plausibility shelters' actually needed, and second, to evolve symbolic language and practices to help Christians 're-enchant their world, redeem their time and recapture the imagination' that places faith in God at the heart of life – creating communities that offer a 'benign sectarianism' where the coherence and credibility of faith is preserved and consistently promoted, but not in a manner that makes it 'alien or other'.[7] In a society where other plausibility structures coexist and compete, it is not enough simply to offer 'answers' to compelling questions; there is also a need to fund imagination and support questions of identity.

Choice, then, presents a particular challenge in faith formation. Young people need to have places that shelter the plausibility for faith and that enable continual checking, evaluation and assurance. Some would see faith and belief as the mere product of a plausibility structure that a person inhabits – or ceases to inhabit – and many who look at 'disaffiliation from religion' would argue that this is all it is. This would not be the perspective of faith formation; but nevertheless the existence and influence of plausibility structures need to be taken into account in our concept of faith formation. Thinking back to Westerhoff, this is exactly what has been suggested as the type of environment required in which faith sharing and the nurturing of faith by the Spirit can occur. The issue for today is that many of these have to be generated: plausibility shelters need to be built to help make faith possible, and within these a focus is needed on developing imaginative Christian practices that enable faith to be held.

Creating Christian place: youth groups as plausibility shelters

Youth ministry groups have a strong history of providing places for young people to hang out, meet with friends, discuss faith and engage in worship or prayer. Some groups tend to be more social and some more spiritual, depending on the young people who attend and the intentions they or the organizing leaders have for these groups. Youth ministry groups are by their very nature intended to be 'in-between places' within a church community or between a church and young people in their community. These

---

[7] Ann Morisy, *Journeying Out: A New Approach to Christian Mission* (London/New York: Morehouse, 2004).

places help to set the group as a centre where young people can gain a sense of distance from the familial influences, and gaze, in a church community and at the same time retain a close connection with the church as a faith community.[8] Outreach groups become an accessible point of contact with the church community either as an extension of social activities to young people or as a deliberate attempt to engage young people in discussion on and exploration of faith. The importance of such places is, however, much greater than the ease of meeting. We need these places to enable young people to make a 'plausible choice' to believe. Places of plausibility are the first requirement for faith generation.

In such places young people are better enabled to address the issue of choice that presents itself as the first challenge of faith in a secular age. It is not surprising that a strong social dimension – especially with peers – is helpful, given that the challenge of choice is one that impinges deeply on sense of identity. However, these places need to be constructed to provide not only a robust enough reinforcement of the plausibility of belief but also a reasonable porousness with the experience of being Christian elsewhere. They need to be able to provide practices that help manage the continual flow between the differing places of plausibility young people encounter. This is crucial to faith generation, as the proximal impact of secularization can be felt if such structures are either too tight or too weak. If they are too tight then young people do not get the opportunity to explore the boundaries of faith, to question their own understandings and build their own perspectives. There is also a need for such places to be provided as an extension to the plausibility shelter offered by the family for Christian young people. For those who have no faith background these places are ones of encounter, where being in a Christian place needs to be tangible. Conversely, though, if these places are too weak then they cease to be beneficial to the task of faith generation.

---

[8] Pete Ward, 'Distance and Closeness: Finding the Right Ecclesial Context for Youth Ministry', in *The Church and Youth Ministry*, ed. Pete Ward (Oxford: Lynx, 1995), 34–49.

Within such places the next challenge of faith generation lies in how practices help to provide a meaningful understanding of faith as identity. Identity is the key issue for these young people, and faith identity in particular. The choice to believe is one that extends to the core understanding of 'who they are'. Choice is not to be negotiated by helping young people make the 'right choice' but by helping them make sense of it as an identity choice. Such a choice is continual and to be managed. The young people I interviewed in Impact and No. 1 are engaged in Faith Identity Work – the task of trying to be Christian involves both initial and ongoing choices around their identity. As such, places of plausibility have to help generate possibility; they do not defend the place of faith in a young person's life but provide a place to help define what this faith might look like. Again the group is pivotal in meeting this challenge. Choice, though, is only one of the key challenges of faith in a secular age, as the next chapter explores.

Questions for discussion

1 Depending on your answer to the questions at the end of Chapter 1, reflect on the ways in which youth ministry from a small base or firm base affects the plausibility of faith for young people in your context.

2 What do you see or hear as the main challenges to the plausibility of faith from the young people you know?

3 Do the distinctions between the Faith Identity Work of young people brought up to believe and those brought into faith ring true in your experience?

4 Identify one possible aspect of a plausibility shelter that can be built in your context.

4

Making coherent sense: forming groups for Christian identity

--------◆•◆•◆--------

I can remember singing during the worship one night and this overwhelming feeling of happiness and comfort came over me. It's like a tingling feeling and I could just tell that it was the Holy Spirit. It was at the point that I fully realized the awesomeness of God, and for me it was the proof of his existence that I had always craved. (Natalie)

If *choice* represents the first challenge of faith in a secular age, and the first impact of secularization that has to be addressed in faith generation, then *sense* is the next. How do we encourage young people whose context is one of a 'happy midi-narrative' to embrace and understand their own sense of self-identity within a bigger story which provides coherent meaning with respect to their actual experience of God in the world and the place of God in their life experiences?

The choice to believe is deeply affected by the plausibility given in communities of faith. However, the influence of our secular age also has a profound effect on fundamental aspects of faith, principally the belief that there is a God, that this God is real and that this God acts in our life and in the world around us. This goes beyond the requirement to choose, because even where such a choice is plausible the question is one of whether our faith is real. That is to say, faith requires a sense of God as real and a real understanding of God that makes sense. The particular challenge in a secular age is both experiencing this sense of transcendence and also being able to name these experiences as a core part of Christian belief. This is a difficult dimension for faith generation as it challenges many of the assumptions that we hold about both the experiences of God voiced by young people and the ways in which they might be interpreting these.

As has already been noted, young people in the happy midi-narrative are not expressly looking for this transcendent reality and may even struggle to grasp and express this. To talk of a 'real' God becomes increasingly difficult, not because, as many might suppose, a real God cannot be rationally argued for, but because experience of God is not part of most people's reality. Experience is not therefore merely 'feelings' or intuition; experience is concrete evidence from our senses that God exists. This is the first challenge of sense.

The second challenge of sense is how young people come to terms not only with the choice to own faith for themselves, but how this belief and life makes sense in the light of the wisdom and values of the secular age in which they are also being formed and nurtured. This is the challenge of 'coherent selfhood' – understanding who we are as people whose identity and understanding of self comes through relation to God. Moreover, as we move on from the basis of this belief to consider its implications for the ways we are to live and act, this sense of self has to be able to be more coherent than that provided by a happiness-focused midi-narrative.

This requires youth ministry to help foster types of experiences that can disclose God, and ways in which understanding around these experiences can be developed. It also requires a more thoughtful consideration of youth groups as rich places for learning, where personal experience of faith is explored and questions of how faith gives meaning to the experience of life are posed, debated and validated.

Sense: making faith real

In discussing how we sense and make sense of God in a secular age the work of Charles Taylor is particularly helpful.[1] Taylor's

---

[1] For a readable summary of Taylor from the perspective of Christian ministry, see James K. A. Smith, *How (Not) to Be Secular: Reading Charles Taylor* (Grand Rapids, MI: Eerdmans, 2014).

main argument about the fundamental shifts in our culture is that 'naïve acknowledgement of the transcendent' and the meaning-making claims of a reality beyond 'human flourishing' have gone. For Taylor, 'naiveté is now unavailable to anyone, believer and unbeliever alike'.[2] What he means by this is that we cannot have a simple trust and acceptance of such a reality any more. The real world we inhabit is about the 'here and now' – what Taylor calls the 'immanent frame'. Where this connects with the proximal impact of secularization is that we are able to hold such a naivety in childhood. Believing in the tooth fairy, Santa Claus and baby Jesus can easily be accepted and is, variously, culturally encouraged, but these beliefs are childish and viewed as such by adults. This dismissive view is, however, not a strict phenomenon. There are many people in our culture fascinated with the 'other' – from aliens to the supernatural – and there are human experiences that point to things beyond us: love, the experience of art, music and beauty. These formative spiritualities are, however, for most people not transformative. When they are, they often remain trapped in the 'immanent frame' – they feed the sense of special place, special friends and above all special 'us'!

The challenge for faith formation, then, is twofold. First, as children become adults, how do we anticipate and address the crisis point, or creeping loss of naivety, that accompanies 'growing up' in a secular age? Second, when faith does take hold, how do we ensure this does not become 'flattened' within our practice and beliefs? How do we continue to keep a sense of a transcendent God when our culture presses us to appreciate as 'real' only the 'here and now' and the material stuff of life?

Faith feeling: believing through experience

A central aspect of the way in which young people brought up to believe describe and evaluate their own personal faith is through personal experience. Marcus puts it like this:

---

[2] Charles Taylor, *A Secular Age* (Cambridge, MA: London: Belknap, 2007), 15–20.

> I'd seen [faith] in other people's life and I'd heard other people talking about it, but I didn't properly understand it myself, because I hadn't ever had a personal 'experience'.

Experience, in the way young people use the term, is a rich concept; it points towards a variety of different meanings and understandings. Marcus himself even puts 'experience' in single quotes in the comment above. The word 'experience', for instance, is used to describe the sense of a whole encounter with God in worship. Experience is also used in a similar way to describe an important event, trip or session that has been influential, or shaped a sense of understanding. It is also used to describe how you learn to talk about, explain or stay quiet about your faith – having the experience to know what to do in those contexts. This sense of feeling faith is very important for the way in which young people in this context talk about their general approach to encountering and understanding God.

What is also crucial is that in many ways experience for young people is the 'ground' of faith – if you don't have it, you haven't got it. If there is no experience of God then there is no God to believe in. This is not, however, mere sentimentality. There is a logic to this that young people are very able to process and make sense of. Natalie puts this succinctly and profoundly in the quote that introduced this chapter, saying that it was an experience of God's presence during worship which *was the point* when she 'fully realized the awesomeness of God', giving 'the proof of his existence' that she had always craved.

Experiences within worship at large events are particularly important to these young people. Susanna summed up the importance of going to such large events as, 'I think the thing is where a huge group of Christians meet, you kind of see that you're not alone', and Marcus as 'a feeling of togetherness'. Yet they also recognize the downside of such events: ''cos there are some times where it just doesn't really click with me, and there are people sort of jumping around, and I just don't really want to jump around' (Simon). There is, though, a known difference for these young people between a good gig and a good worship; one conclusion offered by them on this topic was that in a gig there is a buzz and the crowd, but the 'focus is on the event'. In worship the focus is on God, which could happen in either environment – a gig or a worship event.

There is a sense that events such as Spring Harvest provide a total experience – crowd effect and 'encounter with God' – and both these effects have significance for supporting personal faith. From my observations, sung worship is rather more staid in Impact, as Phillip indicates: 'It's just not the same as Spring Harvest, because people can't go crazy or be themselves, in the worship anyway. So, that's what I always look forward to, in Spring Harvest.' However, worship and prayer within Impact, though without the scale, replicates the opportunities to reflect and engage with God in a variety of interactive ways. In one session, I noted that there was absolute silence in the church building as the young people used a variety of prayer stations. Marcus too recalls a prayer exercise in an Impact session:

> I remember I was sitting in front of the font, at the front of [church], and there was, like, some stones, sort of thing, just on a small tarpaulin. And I can't even remember what the exercise was. But, there was just this feeling that was too – I can't put it into words properly, but that God was there.

Participation in Impact provides young people with 'experiences' of God they identify as critical in moving towards a personal faith. The experience too of 'not being the only ones' who are young Christians that they gain through events, and the experience of being in the group, are crucial to their sense of personal faith identity. One problem in this, though, is that experiencing the 'highs of faith' in such events and their daily school life as a 'low' could exacerbate the negative dynamics of the world they traverse, rather than seeking to unify God's presence in these. Yet by participating in the practices in, or accessed through, the group, these young people are enabled to have the kinds of encounters which they assert to be meaningful and significant. In addition to experience, the group also appears to act as a structure for focusing these experiences towards enabling young people to form a sense of personal faith. This is seen in the way in which leaders guide young people towards traditional rites of confirmation and baptism (as a choice when they are ready) and how such actions are contained within their 'testimonies'.

Feeling faith: the experience of believing

For young people in No. 1, Faith Identity Work includes realizing the implications of the faith they have found and putting them into practice. Sarah talked about this challenge in one of the focus groups where the young people were discussing living out their faith:

> I do find that hard going 'cos, like, I still sometimes go out and just get absolutely snotted [drunk], but it's not a good thing to do . . . My dad – and he understands and that, and he knows that I'm Christian and he's there for me, he's been there for me when I've been in hospital and stuff and all that lot, but my mum, she just don't care, at all . . . she doesn't like care about what I believe in and stuff.

Sarah finds encouragement from a strong emotional connection to the leaders, particularly Tania and Jane. In fact, Jane identifies that she often feels as if Sarah is treating her as a 'surrogate mum'. From Sarah's perspective, she is in a process of realizing faith for herself, almost akin to the process that young people in Impact engage in. This is an aspect of support that the leaders are aware of and they deliberately distance themselves, and lessen the intensity of the young people's relationships with particular workers by drawing colleagues into certain situations and conversations.

Another account of the realization of faith relates to a more 'spiritual' encounter. Nicky talks about how praying with a leader caused a change for him. Nicky is a spiritual boy who had an involvement in Wicca before he came to No. 1. In No. 1 he made a strong connection with Pete, a volunteer leader who had started helping at the drop-in around the same time Nicky started coming. Before becoming a Christian Pete had had a fascination with the supernatural similar to that of Nicky. Pete had connected with Nicky, not in conversation about the supernatural interests, but because he found him crying at the drop-in one day. He asked him what the problem was and Nicky answered, 'I think I want to be a Christian.' Nicky then talks about the profound change that this conversation had on him, especially the prayer that accompanied it:

[Pete] was saying a lot of stuff about 'Help Nicky and, like, help him with this Wicca stuff and help him to get rid of all this baggage he's got.' And, seriously, I closed my eyes and I could just feel his hand, this warm hand coming down and taking all this baggage off me. It was so amazing.

This is a realization that had a profound effect on Nicky. Since then he has been more involved in the drop-in and meeting his discipler (Dominic), but does not go to church.

Sarah and Nicky thus have very different stories about the way in which they have realized the importance of faith to them and for them, and have begun to understand the activity of God in their lives. For both, though, it is the realization of faith, as an understanding and experience of God, that has currency to help them address the issues and concerns they have. This requires nurturing and guiding by the workers, but it represents how their identity work becomes Faith Identity Work.

Making sense: questioning real faith

The second challenge of the immanent frame is to our own theology and practice as people of faith. Put simply, how do we 'allow' God to break into the world we live in and how do we nurture a view of the world that can see this 'reality'? Many critiques of contemporary spirituality address a loss of 'transcendence' or the idea that faith is increasingly becoming all about 'me'. This is part of the 'social imagination' of modern people.[3] What this means in practice is that our theological learning requires the ability not only to make sense of the challenges and questions about the reality of faith, but also the ability and capacity to see things differently as a result of holding to faith.

---

[3] Taylor, *A Secular Age*, 171–6.

A real faith must also give us the capacity to understand the reality of our everyday experiences through faith – to make sense of the world we live in through our Christian understanding. This extends beyond the task of providing a plausible account to defend faith to an experience of faith that begins to transform a person's identity *and* imagination. As in our discussion of the formation of Christian identity, this involves a measure of education, but this is transformative education.

If the understanding of transcendence in our lives becomes increasingly 'flat' as we grow into adulthood, how does God break in as we either experience previous acceptance fading away or never really held this possibility in the first place? In this regard, faith development is not possible any more; faith is an accomplishment in young adulthood. Something new is required to help bridge into this world, or – what is more challenging – something new is required in our formation of children to begin this process. There is a new intentionality and intelligence about children's ministry at the moment whereby 'experience and understanding' is seen as a key to healthy formation. For some this is based on the premise that children don't grow in their faith merely by colouring in pictures of Jesus![4] While this is true, at a more essential level it is about not accepting naivety as enough any more. People need to learn from an early age how to experience God and how to make sense of this.

In order to sense God we need to be deliberate in creating the spaces and practices that enable young people to experience God's presence. This is not necessarily tied to any particular tradition, but is likely to require both a connection to historic Christian practices and a connection to current cultural and understandable reference points. This has been at the heart of the development of youth worship and is increasingly the focus of worship for children and intergenerational settings.[5] At the same time we will need to help children – and especially young people – ponder and

---

[4] Ivy Beckwith, *Postmodern Children's Ministry: Ministry to Children in the 21st Century* (El Cajon, CA: Youth Specialties, 2004).

[5] Pete Ward and Lindsay Urwin, *Youthful Spirit* (London: Tufton Books/The Church Union, 1998).

process what the experience of God in their lives means. This is a particular challenge when it counters both the experience of the 'absence' of God in everyday life and the 'awkwardness' of defending faith identity. It is also particularly difficult in mission contexts where it is accompanied by criticism or questioning from parents.

This links to a further aspect of research on Generation Y, that an expression of spirituality and identifiable experiences of 'something beyond' are often clearly associated with particular spaces or places.[6] The very nature of 'belief' cannot easily be separated from the social contexts which it is connected to. These places often had a story or a purpose attached to them – whether it was a story of belonging in a youth group, or the regular experience of prayer in one's own bedroom. Belief is very hard to separate from that of one's friends and is tied to experiences that are linked to specific places. There is a further depth to these relationships – between key friends and key places. They are also the primary sources young people draw on in the development and expression of their identity.

Seeking sense: places to find answers and raise questions

Friendship and community is a critical aspect of the role of the group. However, what is also evident is that the teaching provided through Impact is appreciated too. This is all the more so because of the experience of the challenges and questions raised around faith through school. The importance of 'learning' is recognized and valued by young people. This was indicated strongly in one of the focus groups involving young people from Impact:

MARCUS   The best thing about Impact is the learning.
GERARD   It's a lot easier for me to learn from Impact than from church.

The boys in this group discussed why this was the case, indicating that they understood that the teaching was 'designed for them'. As Marcus said:

---

[6] Sylvia Collins-Mayo, Bob Mayo, Sally Nash and Christopher Cocksworth, *The Faith of Generation Y* (London: Church House Publishing, 2010), 68.

It's for young people, it's not for everyone, it's not for adults down to babies, which the church is. It's pitching it so that adults can get something from it, whereas if they're pitching it at the ten-year-old level, then the adults are just going to be like, 'Oh, I know that already, that means nothing to me.' Whereas Impact is something that is specifically targeted at our age range.

What is helpful to note here is that this learning offers something more than knowledge and understanding; it doesn't explain principles and practices of belief, but is formative in how these young people feel about their task of being Christian. As two of the boys go on to explain:

GERARD   So that we can understand it, that we can hack it.

PHILLIP   See how it relates to us.

'Teaching' is an element of provision that young people in Impact value and appreciate and they are aware that their youth leaders make this relevant for them. The belief that without this they wouldn't be able to 'hack it' relates back to earlier discussion of the difficulty of being Christian in school; it is not just that they would not be able to 'hack' teaching in church, but that they wouldn't be able to hack being a Christian. This shows how vital the support is. However, what makes this provision operable is not merely the relevance that the leaders can demonstrate, but the fact that these young people are learners. Marcus and Jessica both indicated this in their interviews. For Marcus, small group meetings provide a particularly helpful venue for discussing questions about faith that have been provoked at school:

We discuss the issue of suffering, and stuff like that, and other religions, and those really big questions . . . Patrick [the youth leader] is really helpful, because he knows exactly how to tackle stuff and how to talk things through with you.

Marcus appreciates the small group set-up because it is easier to address questions there than in the larger Sunday night meeting. He pointed out that 'when we have our small groups . . . then we can actually have a proper discussion and we can all ask our questions. And I think those are the times where you really learn stuff.'

Learning also occurs informally in conversation and here the youth leaders are perceived to be 'a resource' by the young people as they seek to gather the understanding they require to sustain the intellectual challenge to faith. Jessica commented in a focus group on what resources the young people had for the intellectual side of their faith:

> Just the youth leaders, actually, like, I remember I would just maybe say, to, like, Patrick, something like, 'What's this about? Why do you say this?' Or something like that, or talk to someone, maybe my parents or something, and then they will kind of explain it to me. I mean, I know there's books and stuff about it, but I don't really read stuff like that.

Learning too comes from other young people and in the ways that young people share their experiences and solutions to dilemmas while asking specific advice from older or more 'experienced Christians' in the group. One example is Hattie asking Colin about how to focus in worship:

> You're so aware of everyone around you. But, then, as Colin actually said to me, just to think that you're in a tunnel, and on top of the tunnel is God, and you're just trying to get up there to him.

(This is an important aspect of the role of the youth group that I will return to shortly.)

Sense making: places to raise questions and find answers

For the young people who drop in to faith, questions around the importance of faith start in the social interactions with the youth leaders and volunteers in the drop-in centre. However, it is within some of the focused intentional activities that they identify transformational learning. One of these is the Youth Alpha programme.

Youth Alpha is seen in the Faith Story data either as the place where these young people made decisions about faith, or an event they want to participate in to help them understand faith. The leaders follow the Youth Alpha programme without much deviation, but it is designed to be discursive and interactive. In addition the team use this space as an opportunity – within the drop-in environment – to introduce Christian practices such as worship and prayer. In an interview, I asked Abigail why she found Youth Alpha helpful. She replied:

> Just like, I don't know, it was just the fact that you were learning more about, like, the leaders' faiths and why they believed it, exactly, like about God and about Jesus and how it all sort of works and how it fits, how Christianity works way more than – there's more proof, to be honest, about Christianity, because it all fits more, nothing else really seems to fit, seems a bit odd – and that all fits and it works, and yeah.

Youth Alpha provides a context where this faith is more explicitly revealed to complement that which has been observed. Further, as Abigail implies here, it provides opportunity to see her faith as 'all fitting and working'. Youth Alpha is crucial in No. 1 to enable a move to personal faith. This is a longer process for some than others. Bryony participated in three Alpha courses, and one of the leaders commented that they were surprised that she eventually decided to become a Christian. As she says:

> At the start of the Alpha course and well I didn't really understand what they were talking about. I have done a couple of Alpha courses now and although I have become more aware of what God is about I don't know enough myself personally to make that step, actually give myself to God.

Youth Alpha was mentioned with affection and a lot of laughter. It has the richness of 'experience' I noted earlier. This is captured in comments like: 'Remember when Martin tried to explain the Trinity with that camera thing [a tripod]' and 'Remember about "the Sausage and the Chicken".' Alpha also creates an opportunity to engage in identity issues. Mark learned things in Alpha – 'We kept getting more information, and I became more and more pleased and interested' – but he also indicated Alpha as a 'place' to address his struggles with anger:

> We did this sleepover in Vicar Church thingy . . . I was kind
> of p – – – – d off and I kind of went somewhere to think, and
> as I came out, Martin was there, and I kind of discussed why
> I was angry, upset, p – – – – d off, and he just sat there and
> described that God could change everything.

Mark goes on to talk about how he prayed with Martin and how
he has felt personally changed by becoming a Christian. Billy too
talks about the importance of praying in the context of Alpha:

> One time at Alpha, there was this day out, we went to the
> cinema and had McDonald's and that, and we came back and
> we had a talk, all of us, and me, Malcolm and Lisa in the room,
> where the PlayStation is, and we just said prayers and just it
> was really nice, it did feel nice.

Alpha provides a key place for the learning, social participation
and experience of God. Each of these makes an impact on the
identity of the young people and is also a place where they are
more enabled to pursue their identity work towards being Faith
Identity Work.

Group sense: ordinary and ordered learning

Providing places of experience and experiential learning is crucial
for the distinctive learning in youth groups – for it to be Christian
learning that is distinctive for young people. However, what keeps
it distinctively Christian is also important. This function of youth
ministry can be seen in the ways in which it is undertaken through
'ordinary and ordered' learning.

Ordinary learning, or 'ordinary theology' as Jeff Astley sees this,
is premised upon 'God-talk among believers who have received
no scholarly education'.[7] Astley frames ordinary theology within
Christian education and suggests that the key term to deploy in
understanding participation in this activity is that of the 'learner' –
where learning entails 'any enduring change brought about by

---

[7] Jeff Astley, *Ordinary Theology: Looking, Listening and Learning in Theology*, Explorations
in Pastoral, Practical, and Empirical Theology (Aldershot: Ashgate, 2002).

experience'. Learning is an expansive activity which includes cognitive learning, but also affective learning through the emotional content and experience of faith, the importance of mentoring relationships (formal and informal), personal critical reflection on experience, the Bible and interaction with other communication within church settings. Astley attributes part of this premise to Farley's notion of habitus, the self-conscious holding of faith as an interpretive stance on life formed in community.[8] Ordinary learning is situated in the whole context of participating and, as has been undertaken here, is best understood by empirical enquiry into the actual settings in which people 'learn faith'. As I will note in a moment, in regard to both groups, learning is not confined to the formal instruction received, or to the informal education that comes through conversations with youth leaders.

Ordered learning relates to the formally designed input in a theological education curriculum. Farley argues that a commitment to 'ordered learning', a systematic approach to outlining the tenets of faith, more usually seen in theological education for ministerial training, should not necessarily be eschewed within the community of faith.[9] With weekly sessions, topics focusing on euthanasia or war, and with a programme of systematic biblical study, these groups are approaching a wide coverage of topics and systematic understanding of faith over the three years or more that young people are involved in such projects. Both ordinary and ordered learning are important in keeping learning distinctive as Christian. Both ordinary and ordered learning are key to the type of catechesis that helps young people to sense God and make sense of faith. To achieve this, though, young people have to be engaged participants in this process, as this final set of insights from youth leaders and young people in the groups illustrates.

---

[8] Astley, *Ordinary Theology*, 9–12, 54.

[9] Edward Farley, 'Can Church Education Be Theological Education?', in *Theological Perspectives on Christian Formation: A Reader on Theology and Christian Education*, ed. Jeff Astley, Leslie J. Francis and Colin Crowder (Leominster: Gracewing, 1996), 31–44.

A sense-able community: youth groups as communities of learning

For young people in Impact, school also raises intellectual questions about faith in raising 'doubts' about there being a 'different side' to the assumptions of faith these young people have grown up with and the answers to the fundamental questions in life that they have grown up believing. Where such questions do not provoke doubt there remains the need for a forum in which to discuss various issues, such as suffering, creation and war. It is crucial to note that this is not to learn the 'correct' beliefs on these topics, but to gain the learning required to face and debate these issues elsewhere. It is in relation to this that Impact is recognized and appreciated as a place of learning; indeed 'the best thing about Impact is the learning'. This learning, particularly through the small groups, is provision that enables critical reflection on faith from experience. Within this, young people are learning about a range of biblical or theological understanding important to a critical appreciation of faith, but through questions and discussions that they are involved in initiating. The youth leaders are seen to be a valuable 'resource' in this regard. Jessica identifies that they are the people to ask 'What is this about?' or 'Why do you say this?'

In discussing their understanding of faith these young people hold to orthodox views on Jesus dying for their sins and the place that the Bible has in their faith. Yet the context within which these beliefs are worked out is one that presents a degree of contingency and critical appraisal of key Christian beliefs. Discussion has boundaries, reinforced by the youth leaders, but is open to be pressed and pursued. Furthermore, many of the themes impinge directly on the decisions and choices that these young people face and the values of the contemporary culture in which they live. The nature of being a young Christian in these contexts is not wholly prescribed, but they are encouraged to 'view the world through "God glasses"'. Occasionally leaders will specifically counter the way in which they perceive young people to understand or express their faith, as seen in the way in which concern over the motifs of God as 'ultimate friend' led to instigating a new programme.

In conversations with the Impact youth leaders, an issue they discussed was the mix of socializing and 'discipleship'-focused activities within the group. On this point, Claire, the youth minister, noted that a problem some years back had been a group that came wanting to just socialize – a trend that she felt might be resurfacing:

> And so we're facing a dynamic of we're saying, we're running a discipleship group, essentially – now, that's the kind of culture of Impact that has been for ten years now, that it's a Christian youth group, and yet they've actually come in thinking we're here for fun and for socializing . . . to say, 'But this is how we're consuming what you're doing, this is how we're using it and shaping it.' And so, I think, that's a tension we have to negotiate carefully.

These leaders understand that young people need to 'consume' activities in Impact, and recognize that being able to enjoy events and activities for fun is important. They are in fact supportive of this and put effort into shaping this. For instance, as youth leaders they give attention to the small details that make activities memorable and help to bond the group – for instance by organizing group T-shirts for the trip to Spring Harvest. They also see their role as ensuring that the group is not too cliquey by encouraging some of the older young people to chat to the newer younger members and to ask how they are getting involved. However, the leaders resolve to work in a more deliberate way with the young people who seem to have made a transition themselves into using the group as a place to come to 'be Christian', and to try to set the culture of the group as focused around developing faith. Claire uses Frankie as an example, saying, 'Frankie, I think, has made that transition, and it'll be interesting to analyse why.' There is a struggle being expressed here to pursue something more through the group, and the youth leaders aren't fully sure what this should look like. That they want to find out more from the young people is in my view an interesting point – not from a sense of 'asking because they should' but trying to find out 'why' Frankie (and a few other young people mentioned earlier) seem to be more engaged in their faith than others. This, coupled with the decision to directly address the issue of motifs about God, indicates that the nature of Christian identity is an ongoing conversation within Impact. Young people in this group are active in pursuing their own learning about what it means to be Christian. The peer interactions are vital in this process, but it is clear that youth leaders are active in shaping as well as supporting this learning community.

A sense-itive community: youth groups as learning communities

The insights from young people and leaders in No. 1 affirm the importance of these places as learning communities, but also underscore the fact that these need to be communities of learning – places where the experiences of young people help to drive theological understanding and practical expression of faith. Here it is engagement in the leaders' experience of being Christian that is important in driving this, as a comment from Steve, one of the workers, indicates:

> When we set up this place, the idea was to build those relationships and, through the lifestyle, be [a] witness . . . so that young people actually started to ask that question, 'Well, hang on, why do they do this? What's different about them?' To see that, actually, our faith, to us, was real.

One incident that captures the intention of this and the way in which young people respond as part of this community is the time when Jane had a miscarriage. Her husband Martin feels that during this time it was like living in a 'soap opera' – that everyone in the drop-in was watching him and Jane and seeing how they would react. However, one of the things that he was really 'blown away with' was the reaction of Ellen and Charlotte. Ellen sent a text message to Martin with a couple of Bible verses (Ellen had only just gone through Alpha at the time). Martin said that he thought it would be something quite trite, yet he mentions how it made a great impact on him. When Jane thanked her, Ellen said that she felt the verses would 'give them hope' and let them know how 'God felt'. Charlotte texted a poem and Martin said that when he started reading it he found it very powerful.

This small incident shows how the community in No. 1 evolves and young people are active within this. They do not only participate as beneficiaries or junior leaders, but show a depth of involvement in being in a community where God is at the centre. This is a process that is shaped significantly by leaders, in the curriculum and provision they establish. It is, though, highly responsive to the involvement and agendas of young people. Ordinary learning is also evident within the way in which young people 'learn' about being Christian through participation as junior leaders in the youth programmes they help to facilitate.

For these young people learning about faith is also significant to their participation. In addition to what is caught or imitated from leaders, Christian beliefs are learned more formally, through the Youth Alpha course and the 'discipleship' system. Coming to Alpha is a rich experience for these young people, providing a sense of solidarity with the other young people in No. 1 who are exploring their understanding of faith, and providing the opportunity to 'find out more about the leaders' faith' and assimilate their views. In this context they gain understanding not only of the central tenets of the Christian faith, for instance having the Trinity explained through an illustration with a tripod, but also how Christianity offers proof and 'fits and works' alongside their current understanding of their own lives and the world around them. In this way, while young people in No. 1 do not exhibit the same pressure to cohere their knowledge and experience of faith with alternative perspectives encountered in school, they do display the need to integrate the intellectual and moral claims of Christianity with their struggles to form faith habitus.

However, a change for young people's sense of participation in No. 1 is seen in becoming leaders themselves – joining with the adult workers, volunteers and older young people as 'junior helpers'. Being a helper in No. 1 is seen as being tantamount to being a Christian, as it is for Monica when a decision to become a Christian is immediately linked to wanting to 'work at No. 1'. For others, becoming a helper is a way they can imitate the values they have experienced in their own welcome and involvement and show interest, care and encouragement to other young people. This has a positive effect in their consideration of what being Christian means and contributes to their own understanding of faith.

Transforming learning for faith: experience in Christian community

Youth ministry has a deep tradition of Christian education, a set of practices that stretches from catechesis to informal education around spirituality, from peer-led group discussions on social and moral issues through to formalized programmes covering issues of faith and practice. This distinctive learning is undertaken to provide young people with the specific spaces and places within which they can share and raise their own questions about faith and within which they can develop a critical appreciation of the choice to believe. One aspect of this distinctive practice is that experience is regarded as central to the learning and formation process and as such youth ministry groups – and the wider network of activities in which they are situated – are established with experience in mind.

A key challenge for faith formation is the 'flatness' of spirituality in a secular age, the trapping of our search for meaning in the here and now – known variously as the immanent frame and the happy midi-narrative. As such, a primary function of youth ministry is to provide the opportunity for young people to experience a sense of transcendence and to seek to understand God as both immanent and transcendent. This is crucial for faith to become formative. At the same time, however, the immanent reality of life is not closed off from faith but embraced. It is through the friendship and community in the group that God is also experienced and understood – belonging *is* believing in this sense.

As learning communities, youth groups possess a quality that distinguishes them from the wider community of faith – or from communities in which faith is not up for discussion. They are places where questions and curiosity are encouraged. At the same time they are creative environments in which the task of being

Christian is openly held and discussed. Crucially this involves some deeper drawing in of the traditions into which they are set in a manner that helps to retain the distinctive quality of these groups as Christian. As will be discussed next, this function of youth ministry is to be a place where the task of being Christian is intentionally held and 'practised'.

Questions for discussion

1 Depending on your answer to questions at the end of Chapter 1, reflect on the ways in which youth ministry from a small base or a firm base affects the capacity to engage in transformational learning.

2 In what ways do you agree or disagree with the idea of an 'immanent frame' in contemporary spirituality and faith? How is this present within church life?

3 In what ways have ordinary and ordered learning been influential in your own faith formation? What have been some of the significant contexts for this?

4 If you are a youth leader, reflect on your teaching programme over the past year. What have you covered and what have been some of the key issues that have been raised by young people? If you're not a youth leader, ask someone who is!

5

Making reliable use: young people being Christian

———•◦•———

Well, it sort of brought the three of us together as friends, by that person. But, it just sort of made me realize, you know, God can throw together a place like this and, I didn't see it then, but the change I've seen in a few people, you know, if he can do that, then he must be real.   *(Ellen)*

In sketching the challenges of forming faith in a secular age, I have identified the challenges of *choice* and *sense* as requiring attention. *Choice* strongly relates to the plausibility, or rather the implausibility, of faith. *Sense* connects with both the need to experience God and the difficulties of making sense of the experience of faith. The third area for exploration is that of *use*. Faith in a secular age has to prove to be useful to a person in his or her daily life. It has to be reliable. This involves not only practices that support young people in negotiating challenges to faith, but also ones that sustain their imagination as people of faith who can perceive and respond to God in everyday life.

The question of faith being useful comes into sharp focus when young people consider whether it really makes a difference in a person's life. Does being a Christian offer a basis to live, and an understanding of life and a sense of identity that is any more meaningful than the alternative of having no faith? Is faith reliable – in the sense that this way of life can be relied upon as we live and work? At the same time, however, to rely on faith in this way runs the risk of Christian faith being reduced to its 'utility' as therapy or a means to ensure happiness. Being Christian is part of a continuing story of encounter and response to God as creator and sustainer of all. In this sense, then, faith also has to be reliable in that it continues in this tradition.

It is through participation in Christian community that a person learns to interpret faith and also learns to interpret the world he or she lives in through faith. This requires the presence of others sharing this journey, but also a clear understanding and connection to the presence of God. This is the formation of Christian habitus – the way in which a person's sense of self as Christian is formed in relation to participation in Christian practices and community. It is this process and how this leads to a reliable faith that I will explore in this chapter.

Working at faith: useful participation

In her book *Transforming Practice*, the theologian Elaine Graham develops Farley's view of habitus not as a 'regulatory object' for a person's faith, but as a descriptive tool for identifying the relationship between faith, identity and practices. This view is strongly influenced by the use of habitus by the sociologist Pierre Bourdieu, but is not specific to the way he uses it.[1] To make this distinction I will use 'faith habitus' to refer to the more general use of the term by Graham and others.

For Graham an important distinction for faith habitus is that when we engage in Christian practice, such as the learning, prayer, worship and fellowship spoken about already, we are not only being formed by the 'moral values and views' these reinforce – expressed theologically or otherwise – but we are also engaging in acts that reveal God and bring transformation at both personal and communal levels. Participation in the practices of faith communities not only enables us to 'indwell our tradition'; it also 'gives rise to new knowledge' and serves to reinforce self-identity. Graham suggests that faith is 'indwelt and constructed: habitus as handed down and re-interpreted anew for every

---

[1] I too am influenced by Bourdieu's use in underpinning my understanding of habitus as the way in which people can be understood to 'carry' views and dispositions and the way in which these are 'held' by the social environments in which they live and act.

generation'.[2] Like Farley, she argues that this is made possible through participation in an intentional Christian community and is observable in concrete pastoral practices. This 'indwelling and construction' is crucial to connect faith and identity and, as I explore in this section, is a function of youth ministry in faith generation.

Faithful participation: the testimony of youth groups

As I have already noted, a key practice for Impact is confirmation. One of the requirements for confirmation is to write a testimony to be included in the service sheet for that event. Writing this testimony is a key activity within the confirmation preparation, involving the youth leader(s) meeting the young people to talk this through, and checking through what is written. This is more than preparing a statement to deliver. The time taken over this process relates to other activities in which 'sharing' is required. These were chances for 'testimony' as young people shared what they thought they could be or could do with their lives. Yet taking time to construct and articulate their Faith Story perhaps plays a significant role in being able to own a sense of choice over faith, to construct their own account of why they are Christian.

In this respect, articulating and sharing a testimony highlights the overall process of indwelling a faith habitus. It represents the fact that the whole activity of the group is centred on being able to 'comfortably' express a sense of self as Christian, from the plausibility given by the group, the experiences of encounter in prayer and worship, and the ordinary and ordered learning. It is, though, constructed. It represents the ways in which young people bring their own meaning and perspective to this account, come to terms with their own story, and identify the particular experiences, feelings or events that are important to them in their faith. This is not to imply that this is somehow a forced or false process, though undoubtedly it could be, merely that testimony is a practice that facilitates this necessary task.

---

[2] Elaine L. Graham, *Transforming Practice: Pastoral Theology in an Age of Uncertainty* (London: Mowbray, 1996), 99–111.

Testimony is also observed as an ongoing practice – the sharing of one's own story and experience of faith with others who 'know'. Simon, for instance, indicated that although his family is supportive of the struggles of being a young Christian, it is the 'people your age, who are going through the same things you are, who can be really more supportive than people who have always done it'. This aspect of participating in Impact is highly regarded by many. For instance, Natalie puts the role of Impact in maintaining her faith identity succinctly in her Faith Story:

> Impact is also a key part to my faith. I find it really helps when keeping me in touch with God, and being able to share your worries, hopes and experiences with others is incredibly important to me.

Sharing worries with Christian friends is in Natalie's experience a crucial aspect of faith. It keeps her in touch with God. Young people in Impact mostly agree that their Christian friends are 'different' from other friends and faith would be harder without their support.

Two aspects of why such friends are important seem pertinent: being able to talk and being part of a group that enables you to feel good about yourself and faith. At a dinner for Impact members, Bruce, a former member and now a leader, was sharing why Impact had been so important to him:

> I think one of the reasons for that is that Impact gives you an opportunity to be somewhere where you can talk about anything that's on your mind. There's no situation or topic or anything that's a taboo or that gets people, I don't know, angry or anything like that.

Earlier Bruce had commented that these people are still his closest friends and though they are now separated by hundreds of miles, 'they're still . . . the first people that I'd be willing to talk to about pretty much anything'. Being able to talk about specific issues with friends appears to be more highly regarded by young people in Impact than talking to youth leaders who, as I will discuss later, are more relied upon for questions about faith.

Participation in faith: youth groups as testimony

The telling of testimony is also part of the activity in No. 1. As in the youth group Impact, this is in part because of the evangelical heritage of the organization. Yet the use of testimony here is similarly constructive, as well as a practice that helps to indwell the faith traditions and understandings of the group. The process here is slightly different in that while baptism (usually in this context) is held as a core practice of expressing the fact that one has become a Christian, and a testimony to accompany this is developed and articulated, it is the testimony – as in witness – of the group and leaders that helps to form the sense of place and community in which to begin to indwell what being Christian means. There is, though, a structure to this process that illustrates an intention that participation ought to lead to an indwelling of faith as habitus.

While learning about the basis and practices of faith, participation in Alpha is also perhaps a 'rite of passage' into inclusion in the core community of No. 1. Ellen indicates this in discussing the importance to her of her Alpha cohort:

> Well, it sort of brought the three of us together as friends, by that person. But, it just sort of made me realize, you know, God can throw together a place like this and, I didn't see it then, but the change I've seen in a few people, you know, if he can do that, then he must be real.

Post-Alpha, young people in No. 1 are paired up with a mentor, or 'discipler', with whom they meet on a regular basis. This relationship is another vehicle through which formal teaching is offered with a programme of topics to discuss. The youth leaders have written this material. It is a 'Christian basics course' with discussion on the Bible and topics such as baptism, grace, the cross and the Holy Spirit. (It was being written during the period of my fieldwork.) Meetings usually happen within the drop-in, but occasionally elsewhere. A focus of this relationship is in supporting young people towards getting baptized and writing a testimony to correspond to this. Again this is flexible: each young person decides when he or she wishes to engage in this, a topic the discipler will discuss. It is also this mentor who helps the young person work through and write out his or her testimony.

Practising use: letting faith work

Indwelling and constructing faith habitus is an active process that requires meaningful participation. This then is the foundation for reliable faith, as it is the basis on which faith and identity genuinely connect. However, it is only one aspect of the relationship and one requirement of reliability. The second area of importance is how useful faith is in life. Here the idea of faith habitus as being able to convey a generative sense of giving both meaning and capacity to act is an important test of faith. This is strongly connected to both the sense of transformation young people experience in their faith, and the way in which this extends to their wider lives. This is not only the way in which particular events – experience of a healing or a worship encounter – become important, but also the way in which participation in the group provides a lifestyle that can support young people as they begin to experience the demands of independent lives.

The idea that young people's lifestyle can convey a sense of agency elsewhere in their lives is helpful in this context because it helps us move beyond an individualized understanding of how faith might help to support identity and a strong sense of self. These are important but it is the participation in the group, and the faith practices, that are also held as valuable. As Graham says, our notion of self in relation to God 'gains substance by its coming into being in concrete, embodied, purposeful practices'.[3]

Young people are understood to be active in fostering their sense of self-identity through pursuing 'youth lifestyles' of cultural and social significance which give them a measure of 'control' over sense of self and provide avenues to respond to their experiences of life elsewhere.[4] This understanding draws similarly on the

---

[3] Graham, *Transforming Practice*, 109.
[4] Steven Miles, *Youth Lifestyles in a Changing World* (Buckingham/Philadelphia: Open University Press, 2000), 60.

concept of *habitus* to draw attention to how our sense of self is influenced by our social and cultural practices. These don't only shape a person's tastes, behaviours and sense of self, but by choosing to associate with others and show cultural preferences, such a lifestyle can be construed as a deliberate strategy to develop identity formed around cultural practices. As noted in the earlier discussion on the happy midi-narrative, young people are already involved in meaning-making activities that can often be as significant and profound as what they find within church – if not more so. Here then the challenge is whether the Christian lifestyle offers this capacity to these young people.

From a faith perspective the idea that participation is crucial does not deny the fact that faith involves choice around belief and a sense of encounter with God. What it affirms is that everyday life as well as religious acts are integral to faith; faith is not learnt doctrine or metaphysical belief, but a lived reality, as Gerrit Immink explains.[5] Faith is an activity located within the social dimension of human life, and this participation is the place where we truly learn about

> pain and sadness ... face disappointments ... experience joy ... the good and pleasant aspects of life ... satisfaction about the progress we make in knowledge and skills ... delight in beauty; and zest for life ... sharing in joy and sorrow is part of life.[6]

Here, then, participation in youth ministry can play a vital role in providing young people with an identifiable lifestyle and a rich social context to share in this dimension of faith. This is where faith can be relied upon.

Relying on God: youth groups as Christian lifestyle

Using the premise of Faith Identity Work to read against other aspects of the data provided insight into how particular motifs about God interact with the necessity and capacity to engage in

---

[5] Gerrit Immink, *Faith: A Practical Theological Reconstruction*, Studies in Practical Theology (Grand Rapids, MI/Cambridge: Eerdmans, 2005).

[6] Immink, *Faith*, 54.

Faith Identity Work. God is seen as a friend, 'to talk [to] about things you wouldn't with anybody else'; God is 'the ultimate friend ... the only person I can truly pour my heart out to' and 'someone to be there in all your decision making'. This aspect of young people's conceptions of God is balanced by the more reverential attitude in worship and data on orthodox evangelical beliefs about sin and salvation. However, the notion of 'God being there for you' appears to help young people to 'use' this relationship in managing the experience of day-to-day life and confronting life decisions.

In the second series of focus groups, young people were asked to explain pictures they had drawn of 'their relationship with God'. One group member described 'a door, and it says, "this way, please" because I just want God to, kind of, show me a direction'; said another, 'Mine's like scribbles ... it's basically meant to represent that I don't really have a way that my life's going at the moment, so, it's all over the place ... and [I've drawn] Jesus right in the centre.' Acting on such sentiments in engaging with God is seen through the way in which prayer is an important activity in managing stress and making decisions. Marcus underscored this approach to prayer, saying: 'If something's really bothering me I pray about it ... I don't know, just have some time alone for myself if things are getting on top of me.'

Phillip talked about a similar personal practice. He stated that he prayed moment by moment throughout the day but also took 'time out' with God, particularly over key stresses like exams or, as happened for one young person in this group, a personal bereavement. Simon talks about managing his moods when he was 'quite depressed and stuff, a lot of the time, and I was quite often sort of complaining to God about that' and that this 'helped me along the way, in changing'. Amelia provides further insight into how praying in this fashion works for her: 'It helps me sort out all the thoughts in my head and helps me keep calm.' There is no sense of direct guidance in this, or a particular conscious understanding of what God is saying, but it is prayer for her and it is important. God 'being there' appears to be enough. However, this is true too within deeper experiences. Alex talks of this poignantly in regard to his experience of coping with his father's terminal cancer:

> It was really painful watching him struggle to live . . . it was at the point that I was praying for his peace – that I realized that God had plans, God had ways, and those aren't always what we want, and I realized that the best thing was to let it pass.

Notice here also the phrase 'God had plans'. In addition to God being there, another motif of interest in Faith Identity Work is trusting in God being in control. This often relates to decision making, but as Alex indicates here, it also helps in coping with painful experiences.

Faith Identity Work, then, represents the activity that young people appear to be engaged in as they come to terms with, and secure, their senses of self as Christian. This activity involves coming to a sense of ownership of a deeply ingrained sense of being Christian and a personal choice and path. It is observed in the way in which young people respond to the challenges to being Christian that they experience in school, which are felt as challenges to self-understanding and not just to beliefs or values. In the face of these challenges, individual young people react differently. What appears to be held in common, though, is the idea that faith – belief, identity, friendship and prayer – provides a way to process and handle these challenges. The challenges of course raise tensions and questions, but these are secondary to the support that faith offers in these crises.

This sense of faith operating to secure and support a sense of agency also relates to their handling of day-to-day stresses and more prominent decisions and crises through their relationship to a God they perceive as the 'ultimate friend'. However, an important aspect to this activity is also clear in the data. Phillip says that in addition to admitting you're a Christian in school you should also 'go to your group and ask them to pray for you or whatever and any problems you have, talk to them about it'. Similarly, in the girls' group the ability to discuss being a Christian, and to maintain that identity, is related to having a strong network of Christian friends as your 'main friends'.

Making faith reliable: learning Christian lifestyle in youth groups

No. 1 is a vibrant place which, as I have already indicated, young people enjoy coming to. For the young people who have become Christians it is also a place where they value playing a part. Becoming a leader, or 'junior helper' as it is termed, does not involve a fixed process. Leaders ask young people to become junior helpers as they get older (over 17) to enable continued participation (as in the case of Sarah), because they volunteer to help at one of the kids' clubs that the charity runs (Ellen) or because they want to help in the running of the drop-in itself (Nicky, Abigail and Monica). Encouraging such participation is an attitude the leaders display; however, it is the young people's motivations for wanting to become leaders that I will now focus on.

In her Faith Story, Monica writes about the time she associates with becoming a Christian. She reported that when this happened,

> I decided to tell one of the workers ... I texted her asking 'Do I have to be a Christian to work at here?' [She replied] 'Yeah you do.' 'OK kool, 'cos I was going to ask if I could start working there!'

For Monica, 'conversion' precedes becoming a leader, but it is clear that there is an aspect in which becoming a 'leader' in No. 1 is a role she associates with 'being a Christian'.

Being a leader also provides a role in which young people enact the hospitality and welcome they have experienced. Abigail gives insight into this:

> Now, as a leader, I have to, like, I make sure I go and speak to a new person and, like, 'Oh, how are you?' and that, because I know what it was like for me when I first arrived, and it is quite scary.

Being a junior helper confers a change of identity within the community at No. 1. When I asked Ellen if being a Christian made her feel different, more confident, she described the positive change she felt in relation to being a leader:

And like when I asked Martin if I could be a volunteer leader, and he said yeah. Normally, I wouldn't stand up to people, but if I have to, like, if people are messing around, and because I have had to, I think it's built my confidence up.

For Nicky, becoming a leader was an answer to prayer:

About a month ago, or maybe three weeks ago, I prayed to God that I could get a bit closer to No. 1 and help a bit more. And I started cleaning the tables, and then, I think it was a Monday, Duncan come and had a chat with me and said, like, 'How would you like some responsibilities?' I was like, 'Yes! I'd love it.'

Though the role Nicky undertakes is basic, it does not matter. He is involved and part of No. 1 and for him this is an answer to prayer.

Such is the importance of these roles that when Sarah was 'suspended' due to an outburst of violent behaviour this provoked a deliberate and conscious effort to change. She now says that she 'leaves that part of her at the door'. She described her strategy as 'a mantra' she would tell herself when she came into the drop-in such that whenever she has had a bad day she can leave this at the door of the drop-in as she comes through it. Being a leader is ingrained in her view of self and she cannot envisage faith without this identity: 'I reckon I would have completely gone off God, because of my non-Christian mates and stuff.'

These changes in role and identity demarcate a different level of participation that has implications for understanding and experiencing God. Ellen talks about this explicitly:

It's great at, like, kids' club . . . they'll ask you questions of your faith, and be able to tell them that, and then they can see where you're coming from, they sort of understand. If you break it down a bit for them. And then you understand where they're coming from, as well. And you can sort – and the fact that you can all share bits about your lives, it really helps.

Being a leader at the kids' club provides a 'stage' for acting out how faith has been passed on to Ellen. It also appears that Ellen is strengthening and deepening her own sense of faith through engaging in this role. Being a leader then provides a 'safe' context within which her faith is 'tested'. Sarah confirms this view in her comments about being a leader in No. 1, saying that as 'leaders' they are 'basically role models for the kids, and the more we get fed by God, the more we can give out to the people, and the more they'll understand it, and stuff'. In this way the young people are modelling and adopting exactly what they have been shown by their leaders.

Faith Identity Work is an activity that begins when these young people start to integrate their personal struggles and general identity work with an emerging understanding of self as Christian. This is generated through participation in No. 1. As a 'Christian place' it is where they encounter a community and practices through which faith is made meaningful and within which they can begin to engage in Faith Identity Work of their own. This is structured and supported by the leaders through having open provision and focused provision. Alpha is a key aspect of this and participation here brings a different dimension to faith with both new understanding and personal experience of God. Becoming a leader is an act of participation that young people desire. It confers a stronger sense of self and enables them to begin to express their own understanding of faith. In the final section I will discuss some of the leaders' views and concerns about managing this process.

Reliable faith: the use of intentional community

In looking at faith in a secular age the challenge of the happy midi-narrative means that care needs to be taken in that much of our culture puts great stock in having individual choice, taking responsibility for our future, working at our problems and so on. The risk in embracing use – especially unintentionally – is that we might easily co-opt God as a tool for our own dreams and desires! As one researcher puts it, for young people faith can become a search for 'selfation', not salvation.[7] The use we

---

[7] Johan Roeland, *Selfation: Dutch Evangelical Youth between Subjectivization and Subjection* (Amsterdam: Pallas Proefschriften/Amsterdam University Press, 2009).

are talking about, then, is not disconnected from the task of being faithful disciples, but one in which being a disciple is amply connected to the whole of life – and a positive facet in enabling young people to gain an increased sense of agency as a result of the identity and resources that come from being a person of faith.

Here the final aspect of Graham's view of *transforming practice* is helpful – that we engage in the 'indwelling and construction' and develop a faith habitus that can inform our identity and agency through participation in 'intentional Christian community'. This aspect is important because, similar to the task of 'establishing Christian presence' and that of providing 'ordered and ordinary learning', running youth groups as intentional Christian communities is an essential theological task of youth ministry groups. It is this intentionality that helps to keep alive the question of what it means to be Christian.

Balance of reliability: faith, family and friends

In talking about young people's sense of faith identity, I noted how certain motifs about God as benevolent friend underscored the ways in which young people interpreted areas of their lives – particularly facing difficulties or decisions. In one of the leaders' meetings I observed, the way in which young people adopt and draw upon these motifs was discussed by the leaders as potentially problematic. The context for this was the death of Alex and Delia's father from cancer. Claire (the youth minister) set the tone for a discussion on this topic:

> One of the things I've always felt with Impact is, a lot of adolescent faith seems to revolve around kind of feeling God, and God's purpose is to serve me and make me feel good . . . it's kind of all about that God serves me and gives me an easy life.

Claire's concern was that a few years previous to Alex's father's death, the brother of one of the Impact members had died in a car crash. In her pastoral care of this girl (Emma), Claire had become concerned that the way in which the faith was being presented to young people in Impact wasn't adequate:

When [Emma] was in the group, two or three years ago, and
her brother died, I think one of the things that I felt came out
of that, probably, the time I spent with her, was just that we
need to offer them faith that says, actually, it isn't about being
made to feel good.

This is an attribute of being Christian that Claire herself says
that she is 'still working on' but she suggests that this challenge is
'meatier', something that the young people will respond positively
to, and better than giving the impression that, 'Hey, God's here
and he's fluffy and lovely and just loves you kids and wants to
make you feel good', and that their youth ministry should be to
'aim for a mature discipleship that says, "I'm called to follow God
in all circumstances"'. The other leaders concur with this, Patrick
saying that the 'buddy Jesus' motif is a problem because it misses
a whole other perspective on the 'God that rules the world',
who is not just a God interested in an individual. Claire jokingly
interjects that perhaps they should be trying to make God seem
'more distant': 'Hey, kids, God isn't interested in a friendship with
you – he's mad with you, he's a judge.' However, the focus for the
discussion moves to how they might address this issue as leaders.
Sally suggests that the problem is that the group do not read the
Bible very much and that the leaders should develop a daily reading programme. However, Claire is not sure that this will work
for these young people, reiterating an earlier comment that Impact
needs to help the young people find a way to 'make faith work
for them, to liberate them from not just seeing faith as going to
church, reading their Bible, but trying to live in a certain way'.
The eventual outcome from this discussion is an outline for the
next teaching programme which is themed around the Gospel of
John and also a decision to try to re-emphasize some of the areas
of redressing 'views about God' within the small groups.

The youth workers in this discussion highlight the aspect of
joint effort that I pointed out in the portrait of practice: they
organize the programme in relation to how they perceive the young
people to be interacting with it. However, this is a contrast perhaps
to the way in which learning is seen as being responsive to the

questions young people bring. It is still responding to a need that has been identified, but that need is for theological education more in keeping with the perspective that the leaders think the young people should have. Ironically, one of the reasons why God is perceived as the ultimate friend is that there are references to this in the songs sung and also within some of the activities that the leaders themselves have structured. For instance, one group work task was organized around the question, 'How has Jesus helped you this week?' It is, however, an indication that the leaders want Impact to be a place where a 'proper' understanding of God can be developed, and this requires the construction of a programme that will orientate this.

Balancing reliability: faith, dependency and depth

I noted on a number of occasions both boys and girls coming to the drop-in to come to find and talk to the leaders, either because something had just happened at school or home, or because they had some other issue they wanted to talk through. The young people describe the leaders in very positive ways in their accounts. For instance, Nicky says that 'they give a lot of advice about every-day situations. They're like guardian angels for me. Every single leader here is someone you can tell a secret and they will keep it.'[8]

As well as being youth workers who provide service, the leaders and young people in No. 1 develop personal relationships. I will illustrate this with what might seem a trivial example. In one session I observed, Abigail brought in a mug with 'Granddad' on it for Steve, one of the leaders. Steve said that she had taken to calling him and his wife 'Granddad' and 'Grandma'. I explored this issue in the leaders' focus group:

STEVE   In the ten years that I was here, I started off as big brother, sort of thing, became Dad, and . . . Grandfather.

MARTIN   Yeah, you . . . those change . . . been around –

---

[8] It is worth noting that such a comment does not mean that such confidentiality would in reality be provided. No. 1 has a variety of policies and procedures in place for handling young people's disclosures.

NICK   And in some ways, one of the things I identify is that, that's not something you've deliberately constructed . . . and it's not necessarily a slight against their parents; it's just that, actually, it's provided another mechanism, another . . . It could be, though.

JANE   I wouldn't necessarily – it *is* a slight –

NICK   What do you think?

JANE   We're now parents to thirty kids, thirty-one.

MARTIN More than that.

SARAH   I didn't really have that relationship with my mum, and stuff, so, I, like, basically – and, 'cos, with Jane, it's like, Jane's there, and she was always there, and stuff . . . I thought of her as like a mum figure, as well. But because I didn't need a dad figure, I didn't want any guys around me, whatsoever.

Relating to young people in this surrogate role is intentional, as Jane indicates. However, there are difficult boundaries in this and connections vary. It also indicates that Sarah at least, and Abigail as well, perhaps, have found strong figures with whom they can connect in their developing of their own self-understanding and independent social identity. One 'worry' expressed by the leaders is that young people become dependent on them, or their faith. This is perhaps a reflection of the strain of this pastoral burden but also comes from a desire to see young people have 'independent and self-reliant faith'. Jane notes:

> One of the problems we do have . . . is because they are so much involved with us as leaders, you then find that they take on your faith, so, all of their faith becomes yours. And that particularly happened with Sarah, in terms of me. Sarah's faith was through me, and she couldn't do anything without talking to me first. So, trying to push Sarah back on to God and say, 'No, it's not me you need, it's God', that's a major thing.

To be able to imitate and depend on the faith of the leaders is, though, a crucial aspect of how participation supports Faith Identity Work. Earlier Martin describes their work as a cycle:

And then, you know, that process starts, people start asking questions, they want to start going on Alpha courses, they start making decisions for themselves, and we're starting the headache of how we disciple them, and then it all starts over again.

Allowing young people to be dependent for a phase, establishing them in the drop-in and then encouraging a more independent faith appears to be part of this process. This is, though, dependent upon young people 'asking questions' and participating.

Intentional Christian communities: youth groups as reliable places for faith

There are a number of transformative practices that can be attributed to youth groups. What lies above this, however, is that youth groups act as intentional Christian communities to enable young people to indwell and construct faith through these practices. What is important in intentional Christian communities is that for this activity to occur, these groups must be active in pursuit of establishing Christian presence, not structuring activity merely to form faith or knowledge, but pursuing transforming practice. Testimony is a central 'gathering' practice in this activity as it plays the part of both the 'formal process for indwelling' and an 'ongoing conversation for constructing' an understanding of the self as Christian.

Youth groups are positioned as places where young people and leaders are engaged in searching for a normative understanding of faith – to seek authentic patterns of Christian belief that are meaningful for young people. The focus on integrating life experience and cultural references is more than a facility for good learning. It is a way in which God is able to be disclosed, made real, within their world and their lives, and the fun and the energy of being together is seen by these young people as a spiritual activity, a way that they carve out space for God in their lives. From the leaders' perspective, this is a community for discipleship, not just a social gathering of young people.

Young people invest in relationships with one another and the leaders in making the group a place that they see as a significant part of their lives. This is crucial in connecting faith as social and vice versa – preventing belief from becoming detached from the everyday. In a secular age, the challenge is to make what is sacred present in the everyday. These conversations and this participation itself is a place of encounter; it is pastoral practice. As young people become more involved in relating in this dimension there are occasions when the 'tables are turned' and they become involved in supporting and nurturing the faith of other members and even that of the leaders. Such an evolving of community indicates that these young people have recognized and invested in being part of a Christian community and that the leaders are sensitive enough to let this foster and flourish. They are engaged in faith generation.

Questions for discussion

1 What places do confirmation or baptism have in the life of your congregation or church? How are young people prepared for this?

2 To what extent is participation in youth ministry in your context a lifestyle? What is the broad shape of this activity – in terms of events, trips and groups?

3 Talk with a young person you know about his or her feelings about the youth group he or she belongs to. Do you get a sense that this young person 'relies' on this group in any way?

4 If you are a youth leader, how reliable do you think your group is in providing a context to faithfully 'indwell and construct' faith? If you're not a youth leader or worker, ask some questions that might help you discern this.

6

The practice of faith generation

When the community of faith begins to recognize that new challenges and conditions call for new patterns of response and praxis, a process of intentional practical theological engagement can be the result. (James Fowler[1])

The Church is continually involved in the task of establishing and re-establishing Christian presence, and as it does this we find different ways of being church and draw on new and old practices to sustain our common life and engage in worship. As the context for being Christian shifts, or as we engage in contextual mission, this task often becomes more visible and more urgent. In the previous three chapters I have explored young people's experiences and the 'challenges and conditions' they face in the task of trying to be Christian. These revolve around the obligation for choice, the need to make sense and the requirement of making use of faith. Failure to address these challenges is the principal 'fault line' in the transmission of faith and the primary mission challenge.

In this chapter I focus attention on the three primary areas of action for which the preceding chapters have provided the evidence. First, there is the need to adopt an approach to young people's faith formation that understands this as a process of *generation*, not development. Second, *identity* is the vital focus of attention for youth ministry, in particular, enabling young people to form a sense of self as Christian – a well-defined faith identity.

---

[1] James W. Fowler, 'The Emerging New Shape of Practical Theology', in *Practical Theology: International Perspectives*, ed. Friedrich Schweitzer and Johannes A. van der Ven, Erfahrung und Theologie, Bd 340172-1135 (Frankfurt am Main/New York: P. Lang, 1999), 75–92 (83).

Third, faith generation for young people is best undertaken through participation in an *intentional community* specifically formed for this task.

From these three patterns for faith generation I will then look at the practices that support these approaches and underpin faith generation. To do this I will highlight the core practices observable in the case studies of Impact and No. 1 – activities and actions associated with the need to provide plausibility, make meaning and give reliability to young people's faith. In each of these spheres I will identify the types of practices that are helpful in faith generation and offer two general practices that will be applicable to any youth ministry context. Lastly, I will draw together these patterns and practices in a flexible model for faith generation to counter and reverse the trends in generational decline.

Patterns for faith generation: ecology, identity and participation

The patterns of response that youth ministry represents involve the need to rebuild the ecology to generate faith, to focus on identity as the grounding for faith and to see participation in intentional communities as the means for this Faith Identity Work. These patterns represent a clear paradigm for responding to the challenge of generational decline and to forming faith in a secular age. To implement these, however, there has to be a clearer acceptance of the paradigm shifts that lie behind these approaches and of the theological insights these patterns identify.

From development to generation: the constructive task of rebuilding the ecology of faith

The first pattern for faith generation involves building. In Impact and No. 1 there is a clear focus on the need to build places where being Christian is seen as plausible, to build communities within which young people can experience God and engage in forming personal faith. In addition, this action is itself to be understood as a process of building – the construction of Christian identity. This represents a key shift that is needed in our approach to faith formation, one that moves away from development to generation.

Seeing faith formation as a developmental process has been core to our understanding of both the processes of faith formation for young people raised in Christian homes and also, to a degree, within mission work with young people outside the Church. Much of this theory has focused on 'development narratives' – such as those proposed by Erikson and Piaget – that are based on understanding how young people develop individual identity, intellectual capacity and moral understanding. Such theorists have strongly influenced the faith development models offered by Fowler and Westerhoff. What these theories have in common is a life-stage model of young people's development that relies on a trajectory of 'development' from child, through teenager, to young adult and adult. This model is highly influential in our approach to work with young people in overt and subtle ways.

In the context of youth ministry as Christian education and pastoral care, there is an assumption that we are essentially 'enabling' a natural growth towards maturity. As young people mature into adulthood we need to help this process include faith. Key figures such as Westerhoff underline the fact that faith is not 'natural' and Christian education does not 'move' people from stage to stage. The assumptions of this approach often belie this fact. The assumptions of faith development are damaging for the new conditions we face and, as such, this language is no longer helpful.

Developmental theories have some descriptive value as it is recognized now that the end goals of any developmental stage relate very strongly to the cultural values attributed to the move from childhood to adulthood. These may once have been easily identifiable and largely stable. The German theologian and Christian educationalist Friedrich Schweitzer argues that the demands of a secular age suggest that 'developmental' approaches to faith forma-tion hold limited value. Youth is no longer a stage through which we pass, but a phase of life that contains within it the key aspects of secular culture – it is where we first encounter the plural con-texts for understanding who we are and begin to recognize that holding together our sense of identity requires work and that who we understand ourselves to be is deeply associated with the intentional and intimate relationships we form. We do not transition from this 'life stage' – we learn to live with it. Schweitzer summarizes this challenge as 'how to come to terms with a life cycle that presents itself like a permanent construction site, with an overabundance of competing construction plans and with no clear criteria for choosing among them'.[2]

The demands of the postmodern life cycle are such that 'finding faith becomes a lifelong project'.[3] As such, the formation task in earlier phases of life is one of learning how to hold faith for the rest of life. Faith formation is not only a personal choice but also a choice chosen again and again. How then do we help young people to choose and keep choosing to believe? We need to embrace *construction* as a pattern of practice. First, we have the structural task of constructing places to be Christian: creating groups, events and a network of activities and places that rebuild an appropriate ecology of faith where understanding and experiencing God is plausible. Second, within this we need to focus on the task of constructing an appropriate intentional Christian community where young people can undertake the constructive task of faith generation.

I stress these requirements again not to emphasize their importance – which I have already established – but to stress the importance of being active in building such an ecology and active in making these places where young people are involved in faith generation. This shift requires us to be radical in developing youth groups, congregations, types of churches and projects for young people.

There has been much recent debate about whether youth groups can be considered as youth congregations and whether youth congregations can be considered as church.[4] These are important issues to wrestle with, but I am going to sidestep them. A youth

---

[2] Friedrich Schweitzer, *The Postmodern Life Cycle: Challenges for Church and Theology* (St Louis, MO: Chalice Press, 2004), 17.

[3] Schweitzer, *The Postmodern Life Cycle*, 133.

[4] Graham Cray, *Youth Congregations and the Emerging Church*, Grove Evangelism Series (Cambridge: Grove, 2002).

group may or may not be considered a church in its own right or it may very clearly be a small group that meets as part of a larger congregation – this does not matter! What matters is that the place that is created is understood to be contributing to the task of establishing Christian presence in a particular location with a particular group. Moreover, if there is not some form of capacity within a 'church' for young people to engage in the tasks they need for establishing Christian presence then this contributes to the reduction of plausibility and the weakening of choice to pursue faith.

Similarly, a mission project might be considered to be a Fresh Expression, but in claiming this it too has also to be sufficiently placed to act as a plausibility shelter where faith is generated, not merely nurtured. In this respect the developmental paradigm by which spirituality can be encouraged towards faith is similarly challenged by a faith generation approach. Here, then, projects that aim towards renewing a missional approach to church for young people have an advantage, in that they can help young people to 'encounter' Christian places within which the constructive task of faith generation is more adequately supported.

Rebuilding the ecology of faith and places to be Christian is, then, a strategy to provide the best places, not to nurture or develop spiritual understanding and faith, but to generate this. Such an approach cannot be effective without appreciating and seeking the presence of God to be at work in such places. What we are seeking here is what James Fowler describes as the task of 'enabling Christian presence in the world' – 'an unfolding future, with instincts and imaginations shaped by memories of God's faithful action in the past, and experiences of God in the present'.[5] We do not yet have enough of such places, and they need to be built.

Constructing Christian identity: forming sense of self as Christian

The second pattern for faith generation requires a clearer focus on a theological understanding that faith today is an issue of

---

[5] James W. Fowler, 'Practical Theology and Theological Education: Some Models and Questions', *Theology Today* 42, no. 1 (April 1985), 43–58.

identity as much as belief. Putting this another way, belief is held and expressed as an identity choice, and as such the pastoral-mission focus of our youth groups needs to attend to this task. As discussed previously, this has to be done collaboratively with young people. Faith generation requires that faith identity is 'indwelt and constructed'.

Placing the indwelling and construction of Christian identity at the heart of faith generation is a paradigm shift in faith formation, not because young people's identity formation isn't recognized as important, but because it is not sufficiently attended to in practice. This is partly because our underlying philosophy for many Christian practices – prayer, worship, baptism, confirmation, Communion – assumes that these practices do, through their very nature, contribute to form Christian identity. It is also because the idea that we should encourage the construction of identity is not one that has been traditionally developed in a theological understanding of Christian education and formation.

The affective, moral and intellectual dimensions of belief have been key to the faith developmental theories by means of which we have tried to explore and explain how faith adapts and evolves as we grow through childhood to adulthood.[6] Such theories already recognize this journey as a complex task, one in which faith as a matter of personal identity is a key component. Family remains a key aspect of young people's identity – what is called 'ascribed' identity. There is, though, an increased recognition of the import-ance of the 'achieved' identities that young people form. The issue of identity is not only of theoretical interest; it is also an issue at the forefront of many young people's own expectations and anxieties, as we saw through their comments. What is lacking, perhaps, in faith development theory is a closer consideration of how a person's identity is 'constructed and contested' and how the construction of Christian identity can be generated.

Within youth ministry Kenda Dean directly addresses the issue of identity as crucial to youth ministry in arguing that youth ministry has to aim towards facilitating the formation of

---

[6] James Fowler's theories being prevalent among these.

an identity orientated around the 'passionate identity of the triune God'. However, Dean sees the idea of encouraging young people to actively construct their identity as undesirable and untenable, stating that 'the time-consuming chore of integrating the "me's"' often associated with notions of a patchwork or constructed identity is essentially futile and spiritually dangerous.[7] Dean prefers instead to see the challenge of formation of human identity as finding a 'focal point' or 'core' and suggests that this ought to be regarded as a 'gift' found in Christ, rather than an identity to be attained. However, if one follows the logic of faith as being both gift and work there is a comparable approach to the issue of identity. Young people gather and gain their sense of Christian identity. This requires the freedom to explore their sense of self and how being Christian contributes to this.

As noted above and seen in the experiences young people share about trying to be Christian, there is a strong argument that a person's sense of religious identity is formed in relationship to the different 'worlds' a person inhabits. The construction of Christian identity has to respond to this plural context. What is important for faith identity, then, is to develop a coherence around being Christian – a connection between ascribed and achieved identity – a clear sense of who I am in relation to the different person people expect me to be, or the different people I could be in these different worlds. Here, then, faith identity might be seen as the point of stability for 'holding ourselves together'.[8] This challenge of coherence is key for young people who have been brought up in the Church. For young people who connect with faith from a different background, being Christian offers a new way to understand who they are.

How Christian identity is constructed then needs to take into account the ways in which young people are already going about this task. This is outlined well by Savage, Collins-Mayo, Mayo and Cray in their analysis of the worldview and faith of Generation Y.

[7] Kenda Creasy Dean, *Practicing Passion: Youth and the Quest for a Passionate Church* (Grand Rapids, MI: Eerdmans, 2004), 62.

[8] E. B. Anderson, 'A Constructive Task in Religious Education: Making Christian Selves', *Religious Education* 93, no. 2 (1998), 173–88.

Here they affirm that since young people draw self-identity from narratives and participation in consumer and media lifestyles, the Church needs to have an understanding of spirituality and faith formation that adopts a constructive stance to match this. Young people see themselves as the authors of selfhood; it is not 'a sin' to do so, nor is this some heretical notion of identity formation. If there is a critique of this construction of identity from the Christian tradition it is that these sources of selfhood are drawn upon without reference to God. To redress this, Savage et al. encourage a view that mission needs to offer stronger grounds for constructing identity within the narratives and praxis of the community of faith.[9] What I would add to this insight is that this is similarly true for young people who have been 'brought up to believe'. In this situation these young people are equally in need of clear narratives and practices for identity construction, which is what youth ministry is able to offer as a pattern of church life.

The second shift in appreciation of the central task of faith identity is that this is not only a task to achieve, but also ongoing work. A sense of *coherence* gained through practices that help young people to form faith identity does not lead to a permanent 'achieved' identity, because faith identity is constantly being challenged. The conflict of holding Christian identity in difficult contexts – as we saw in the expressions of young people whose Christian identity involved keeping their 'faith on a safety catch' or switching to 'going all Christian' – requires similar constant support. Added to this, an intellectual, or conceptual, challenge to faith is similarly felt as a challenge to identity. The basis of choice to believe, the incredibility of belief, the hypocrisy of the Church, the negative role of religion, the disproving of faith by science, and similar issues, can be addressed, but they also impact the sense of self. These are all very personal as well as intellectual chal-lenges for young people to grapple with. What is required in this task, then, is *confidence* to match an internal sense of coherence.

---

[9] Sara B. Savage, Sylvia Collins-Mayo and Bob Mayo with Graham Cray, *Making Sense of Generation Y: The World View of 15- to 25-Year-Olds*, Explorations (London: Church House Publishing, 2006), 156–70.

This confidence comes from both the social and spiritual support of the group and the ordinary and ordered learning that takes place within this community. Without this type of group young people can of course still have the experiences of prayer and worship that affirm their faith and can still experience the learning that helps to explain – to themselves and others – why they believe what they believe. Yet it is better to focus attention on a pattern of church life that can provide this intentional community in which they can participate.

Participating in intentional community: constructing ongoing faith

The final pattern of practice that youth ministry helps to establish is one where participation in Christian life and lifestyle is *meaningful*. Young people's participation in church – or mission projects that extend Christian presence – must attend to the questions and issues that young people have. This is an ongoing task that involves first of all finding the practices to help young people deal with the stuff of life – drawing their relationship with God into the process. This, though, cannot stay at the level of 'managing stress' or 'maintaining happiness'. Practices of prayer, worship and nurture need to inform and sustain a worldview that allows them to live in the reality of a 'faith-full' world. This is not an easy task in a secular age where this reality is misunderstood and undermined. Faith generation requires practices that help 'make God known' and help young people to make faith in God central to their lives. This is best achieved in an intentional Christian community that understands and attends to this task. Such groups are not likely to be the larger church communities in which young people are also participants. They are unlikely to be provided by smaller communities in which young people might be encouraged to participate. Such groups are also highly unlikely to be encountered by young people unconnected to church, that is, unless these intentional communities are deliberately formed and participation is actively sought.

As outlined in Chapter 1, my approach to understanding faith is one that requires an understanding of the human and divine aspects of this life – the life of faith. Faith generation requires intentional action, but this action has to be such that it aims at and achieves participation in the life of God. Without this we will not see faith, as we would rightly understand this in a Christian context. This is not to suppose a particular tradition or type of expression; this can and should vary. What needs to be firmly established is that faith generation is not a matter of technique, nor does it rely on imitating things that seem to work. Faith generation is a practical theology of cooperation to provide the conditions for faith to be formed and thrive. This involves young people being able to centre and confirm their faith identity through practices that help to manage this constant 'checking'. It also requires a focused attention on helping young people explore and come to understandings in the areas of faith that raise questions or challenges. Faith is formed as a 'gift and work' in these activities, and to facilitate this requires intentional action. Participation in youth ministry groups not only needs to attend to how young people make sense of their story and make sense of their faith. It also requires generative practices that lead young people into who they are becoming and who they might become.

Forming youth groups as intentional Christian communities is a pattern that requires more conscious attention. In Chapter 2 I explored how youth fellowship groups and relational youth work projects developed a parallel focus on the importance of intentional relationships in pastoral and mission work with young people. The pattern of intentional communities affirms this approach, but adds an additional dimension.

The intentionality of these groups is a pattern that has already been covered. That these groups are Christian, though, is an aspect of their importance that is easily overlooked. When forming a church youth group, or a youth work project connected to the Church, the issue of how this might be distinctly Christian is a key characteristic of the reason these groups exist – they are not social spaces for young people in a church to gather, and they are not open youth work underpinned by a faith ethos. They are intentional communities of practice that seek to wrestle together with what being Christian means – in relation to the challenge this poses for young people who have been brought up to believe as well as for those who have been brought into belief.

In intentional Christian community young people are invited to explore and establish their sense of self and identity within the Christian story and through practices that aim to make God known and knowable. Young people and young adults are more than capable of self-organizing around such a purpose. However, where this is aided and facilitated by a worker or coordinator it can often be better harnessed and directed. This, then, is one reason why employing such people results in a better chance of faith generation. For mission work it is practically essential that a team should have this intention undergirding its work, and that in inviting young people to participate the basis of this involvement is open and transparent.

The association between youth ministry and growth is not co-incidental. Through these patterns of practice, youth ministry attends to the key challenges that contribute to generational decline. The influence of these patterns is to attend to the task of faith generation as an active requirement for a secular age. Where this is done well, it will include attention to rebuild an ecology to support the task. This ecology, as I will discuss later, has implications beyond the direct impact it has on the young people it is intended to serve. This intentional work will, at some level, give recognition to identity as the key to faith generation – a pattern that requires a more conscious and deliberate focus. Lastly, there will be an understanding of the importance of participation as a pattern that underscores all practice – from teaching and learning, to leading, to physical involvement in worship and prayer activities, to the shared task of pastoral care. Learning this approach to being Christian is a foundation not only for forming faith, but also for holding faith in a secular age. This means that the young people who are participants in such groups are more likely to become young adults who participate in establishing Christian presence in their churches. So how do we encourage these patterns? What are the practices that we can establish to make faith generation happen? Is there a model of faith generation we can use to help evolve and establish youth ministry for faith generation?

Faith generation in practice: building plausibility, constructing identity and establishing reliability

In this section I will outline a model for faith generation based on the exploration of young people's participation in youth ministry in earlier chapters and the patterns for practice outlined above.

A model helps people to visualize something larger and more complex than it can actually convey. As Christine Grapes states, 'a model will always be a bit unreal because it is a simplification and a generalization'; the youth ministry models she expands upon 'are presented for guidance, imitation and translocation across diverse settings'.[10] This model is offered in this spirit and to spark debate on what deeper understanding and what fuller practice is actually required for faith generation.

Faith generation requires a set of connected practices that contribute to making the implausible choice to believe, making sense of Christian identity and making reliable use of faith, and can be imagined as a set of connected circles (see Figure 2).

These practices lie at the heart of the intentional communities in which young people participate to indwell and construct Christian identity. These sets of practices build on the interventions youth ministry has already been integral in developing – distinctive learning, intentional relationships and transforming practices. Setting the outcomes required for faith generation as plausibility, identity and reliability gives new grounds upon which these practices and new interventions can be brought into the service of faith generation. Before looking at these three spheres, the approach I am advocating requires a little further explanation of what I mean by the term 'practices'.

---

[10] Christine Grapes, 'Developing Contextual Models of Youth Ministry, Part 1', *Youth and Theology* 4, no. 1 (April 2005): 67–81 (68).

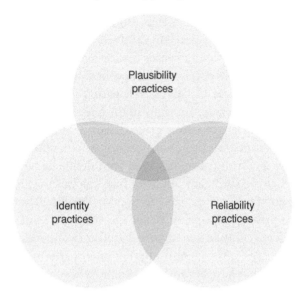

Figure 2 The set of connected practices contributing to faith generation

Faith practices and faith generation

As identified in Chapter 2 there has been a resurgence and recognition of the importance of practices in faith formation, and in youth ministry in particular. This attention often centres on 'Christian practices' and the way in which young people's engagement in these is formative. This is part of the picture, but not the complete set of practices I identify in faith generation.

In affirming a practice approach to faith formation Dykstra and Bass write of Christian practices as 'things Christian people do over time to address fundamental human needs in response to and in the light of God's active presence in the world [in Jesus Christ]'.[11] For Dykstra and Bass such practices are not simply activities that such communities happen to engage in, but the way in which the transformative hope and power of God is mediated to

---

[11] Craig R. Dykstra and Dorothy C. Bass, 'A Theological Understanding of Christian Practices', in *Practicing Theology: Beliefs and Practices in Christian Life*, ed. Miroslav Volf and Dorothy C. Bass (Grand Rapids, MI/Cambridge: Eerdmans, 2002), 13–32 (18).

and encountered by human beings. Human sin may, though, skew practices to become self-deceiving and self-serving so that actions that claim to be purposed towards disclosing and participating in the life of God may in effect do the opposite if they are not 'attuned to the active presence of God'. Participating in such practices is an attempt to participate faithfully in the ongoing activity of God.

An alternative appreciation of Christian practices is provided by Kathryn Tanner, who sees practices not as inherently 'Christian' but as ways in which communities of faith define being Christian through historic Christian practices that are 'born again to new purpose'. For Tanner, Christian practices are flexible, accommodating the reality of organizing social life through contemporary means and engaging in acts signified as historically meaningful.[12] This gives space for the identification of other patterns of practice in church life that have become important. What Tanner also adds is that this makes theological reflection around these practices the central process within a community. Tanner argues that it is the meaning-making value of Christian practices, the way they help form a reflexive habitus of faith, rather than an internal 'property' of practices themselves that is important to embrace.[13]

The practices that I advocate we focus on and develop are three overlapping sets that cover plausibility, identity and reliability. In each of the areas of practice I highlight a centring practice that can be attributed to a historic practice and one that is an example of youth ministry's capacity to use the everyday culture of young people towards faith generation. Each of these spheres of practice is focused on the indwelling and constructing approach articulated above. In this summary I have named practices that the case studies illustrate well. These are not the only practices that can be linked to the tasks of plausibility, identity and reliability. The

---

[12] Kathryn Tanner, 'Theological Reflection and Christian Practices', in *Practicing Theology: Beliefs and Practices in Christian Life*, ed. Miroslav Volf and Dorothy C. Bass (Grand Rapids, MI/Cambridge: Eerdmans, 2002), 228–42 (230).

[13] Tanner develops this further in discussing the meaning-making capacity of Christian cultures and specifically how this is achieved through 'everyday theologies' within which these interpretations are formed; see Kathryn Tanner, *Theories of Culture: A New Agenda for Theology*, Guides to Theological Inquiry (Minneapolis, MN: Fortress Press, 1997).

invitation in this model is to name and develop these as appropriate to the variety of contexts in which such work with young people is undertaken.

Plausibility practices: making distinctive Christian places

This first set of practices revolves around the need to address the challenge of choice and the lack of plausibility. As assessed in Chapter 3 the implausibility of belief challenges all aspects of faith – understanding, social connections and identity. The investment in creating groups, developing places to meet, putting on events, taking trips to events, and going on pilgrimages and to conferences are all vital aspects of youth ministry because they counter this impact. To not do so is to fall into the trap of 'developmental faith' rather than faith generation.

The second practice is the acceptance and fostering of group-faith. In faith development terms *groupfaith* is perceived as a stage through which one 'should' pass to *owned faith*. While in his theory Westerhoff proposes that each layer of faith is not left but added to, in practice this is misdirected. What is apparent in the experiences of young people trying to be Christians is that group-faith and owned faith remain intertwined and interconnected. We cannot then hope for a personal, owned faith without setting in place practices that encourage groupfaith.

Presence: establishing Christian places

Among the assets we have as the Church – in many denominations – are buildings. While some Christian youth work is best undertaken by engaging young people in their spaces,[14] most can make use of the abundant spaces we have available in our buildings, if we choose to make them accessible and appropriate for this use. Building places of plausibility in these spaces, though, takes time and effort.

In the two case studies, both Impact and No. 1 have a distinct space in which the groups meet – one that can also be shaped by the young people who go there. This may seem a trivial and obvious

---

[14] See Richard Passmore, Lorimer J. Passmore and James G. Ballantyne, *Here Be Dragons: Youth Work and Mission Off the Map* (Birmingham: Porthouse, 2013).

observation. It is, however, of great significance – whether the space is a balcony area, a youth room, a drop-in, a bus stop or a whole church building. Dedicating a space where activities and programmes are based is a vital part of presence practices for faith generation. Places, though, are more than spaces in buildings or on streets. It is the association of the space, the people and the interactions that is import- ant in creating places. The techniques and tools for this are not specifically Christian – they are standard aspects of youth provision. Indeed care has to be taken around associations with church or Christianity depending on the group the place serves. The central issues are ownership and identification in this being 'their' place, and autonomy and freedom of expression in the use of such places.

The subtlety with this is that from the outset such places also need to be conceived and constructed as sacred places – places where meeting with God as well as one another is undertaken or at least observed. Such places embody the task at hand as their design and decoration should physically represent the task of con- necting faith and cultural identity.[15] This will look different for different groups of young people. A church-based group will have a higher likelihood of meeting in a small corner, a basement or another identifiable space in a church. This means that the decor and set-up is less likely to need to reflect this and more likely to reflect the individuality of the young people. Yet this space should also be used for prayer and worship as well as social meeting and group work. Young people in mission projects can often come into a church without any connection to the sense of place this has as a church. Here, then, one might want to accentuate that aspect of the space, encouraging young people to meet in parts other than 'the basement' or 'the back'. There is strong evidence that young people do identify with churches as places for them, and have strong associations with their significance as places of worship, but often feel 'unwelcome' in these places.[16] In both cases

---

[15] Sally Nash, Sylvia Collins-Mayo and Bob Mayo, 'Raising Christian Consciousness: Creating Place', *Journal of Youth and Theology* 6, no. 2 (2007): 41–59.

[16] Ruth Dearnley, 'Church Hall vs Lychgate: Which Young People Should We Focus Our Mission Efforts On?', in *Young People + Mission: A Practical Guide*, ed. Alison Booker and David Booker (London: Church House Publishing, 2007), 133–45.

the creation of such places needs to be something that young people are involved in helping construct. Places do not consist only of a physical location; they also have meaning attached to the purpose for which they are used. Here the next practice of *groupfaith* is vital for helping to set this intentionality.

Groupfaith: collaborative catechesis

The challenge of faith generation requires a fresh appreciation of the ways in which we envisage and draw upon the youth group as intentional Christian community. In the mission-focused work of relational youth work, intentional relationships guide the way in which workers engage with young people to nurture interest and exploration into the meaning of the gospel and into ways of exploring and affirming these meanings in worship. As the challenge of faith generation becomes more generally apparent it is evident that such an approach is entirely applicable for young people connected to churches. In the mission context, the challenge is to keep these intentions focused on this task.

The two case studies that were presented above were replete with examples of the group as the primary place of learning and expertise in how to negotiate the task of being Christian. As Marcus stated, young Christians need to 'look for something like Impact, 'cos that will help you more than anything you could know'. In No. 1, Mark (as well as others) articulated the feeling that without the people at No. 1 he would have lost his faith. As discussed in Chapter 4, both groups have established a range of meaning-making practices connected to ordinary and ordered learning about faith; this is collaborative catechesis.

Bible study groups, the Youth Alpha course, programmes of topic-based discussions, one-to-one discipleship relationships and the intentional use of informal conversations to provoke reflection are all forms of learning; what connects them to the task of mean-ing making, though, is to allow the space for this learning to be collaboratively set. In many respects this mirrors the process of indwelling and construction itself. There is an invitation to indwell the traditions and understanding of Christian faith and practice, and to wrestle with how this is understood and enacted. At the same time there is the need to respond to the presenting questions and concerns that young people might have about a particular experience, issue or concern and to construct learning around this. Placing this in the group setting has an affirmed sense of plausibility – you're wrestling with these issues with others wrestling with these issues. You're undertaking catechesis in the context of choice (see Figure 3).

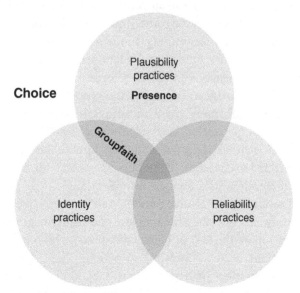

Figure 3 The importance of presence and groupfaith as plausibility practices for facilitating choice

What can be gained through good youth groups is a capacity for theological reflection – a capacity that is not only a recognizable attribute of a mature faith but an increased requirement for faith in a secular and pluralist context.[17] Theological reflection enables the connection of experience to understanding and is also crucial in how our experience and understanding of God evolves. It has been noted by Kenda Dean that most young people might be considered to be 'intuitive theologians'. Young people in

[17] Jeff Astley, *Ordinary Theology: Looking, Listening and Learning in Theology*, Explorations in Pastoral, Practical, and Empirical Theology (Aldershot: Ashgate, 2002).

contemporary culture traffic in theology on a daily basis, through the religious symbols that proliferate in popular culture and through participating in meaning-making rituals that are part of secular youth cultures. Young people who have been raised in a Christian family might also have an 'embedded' theology where they have 'adopted, but not critically examined' faith. What theological reflection can help generate from this intuitive or embedded position is a deliberate theology, one of faith seeking understanding.[18] Youth groups have a role therefore in helping to form this capacity in depth.

When you examine a well-founded youth work programme over the period of time a young person might participate – say three years – it can look very similar to the period of study in theological college. While it may not use the same language and structure, the way in which a youth group might explore the Bible, explore and discuss their understanding of who God is, and seek to make God known in practical ways has more in common with the experience of theological college than that of 'church'. Youth ministry groups that are led well will often cover substantial ground in the theology they engage in; this is often prompted by young people themselves because they need to know the answers to crucial questions to have confidence in their choice to believe. The passing on of the tenets of faith is an essential part of catechesis; in youth groups this is done in a manner that often allows for questioning and wrestling with the process. This is not transmission of faith as a one-way process, but an iterative process. This approach embraces all the facets of distinctive learning, intentional relationships and transforma-tional practices, and works with these towards the intention of moving youth groups to be places where this understanding and meaning making can be achieved. Such action is a crucial aspect of building plausibility and supporting faith identity. In the next section we will look at the practices that contribute further towards the task of indwelling and constructing faith identity.

---

[18] Kenda Creasy Dean, 'Theological Rocks – First Things First', in *Starting Right: Thinking Theologically about Youth Ministry*, ed. Kenda Creasy Dean, Chap Clark and Dave Rahn (Grand Rapids, MI: Zondervan, 2001), 15–39 (29).

Identity practices: meaning making for Christian identity

In Chapters 3, 4 and 5 the issue of faith as identity and the recognition that Faith Identity Work is required to achieve and manage such a sense of self were key insights from the experience of young people trying to be Christian. The challenge of holding and expressing Christian identity connects to the broader challenge of the implausibility of faith, particularly in relation to the other spheres of young people's lives. More specifically, we noted that young people who have been brought up to believe have particular requirements in this regard. Their Faith Identity Work revolves around the need to achieve a personal understanding of faith identity, in order to build on that which has been ascribed to them in childhood. For young people who have dropped in to faith the challenge is similar but distinctive. Their identity work requires integrating faith into their sense of self-understanding.

As discussed earlier in this chapter, placing a focus on the construction of identity is one that has both advocates and detractors. In some respects the basis of understanding whether a person has a 'centred self' or a 'plural self' is immaterial. What matters is whether he or she has a Christian identity that emerges from this sense of self. To achieve this, youth ministry needs to develop – or focus on – specific practices to help support this process. In the explorations of the work of Impact and No. 1 two core practices are seen as important in this task. First was the telling of *testimony* and second was the importance of experiential *encounter* (see Figure 4 on p. 140).

Testimony: coherent faith sense

The practice of 'telling testimony' has become a key feature of evangelical tradition, but has a precedent that goes much further back in church history.[19] Testimony, though, is more than a confession of faith – it links together the understanding of personal faith identity with what it personally means to describe oneself as

---

[19] See Mathew Guest, *Evangelical Identity and Contemporary Culture: A Congregational Study in Innovation*, Studies in Evangelical History and Thought (Milton Keynes: Paternoster Press, 2007), 114–17.

Christian. Testimony is not a private process either – it is inherently public and as such connects this personal understanding with participation in intentional Christian community. Testimony gives voice to how a young person has 'indwelt and constructed' his or her own sense of faith identity.

The groups young people participate in structure the process of shaping and telling testimony. These reflect the tradition these groups come from, but in preparation for baptism or confirmation all denominations have some element of testimony that is required. What is different here is that testimony is not the gathering of an account – a statement of confession about a faith decision. Testimony is a process for either securing or shaping this decision. Work in the broader field of youth studies indicates that supportive work around a 'coherence narrative' can be a positive support for young people in the complex decisions and choices they face.[20] Kerry Young, who writes about youth work practice, suggests that work to support identity formation is a defining feature of modern youth work.[21] There are a variety of ways this is undertaken, for instance: creating a 'who I am box' that contains photos, objects and drawings; writing timelines of where one is from and where one might want to go; writing a letter to a younger self about decisions and regrets; and so on. Here, then, testimony as a series of activities and a final account connects this type of youth work practice with the Christian practice of testimony associated with a faith decision in baptism or confirmation.

Testimony is not only a one-off event but a continual practice. Telling testimony is seen in everyday conversation, in the way in which young people discuss their experiences of faith among friends. Dori Baker, who has investigated the power of testimony as a youth ministry practice, describes this ongoing activity where young people venture personal feelings and thoughts raised by group discussions and give tentative answers when questions such

---

[20] R. Devadason, 'Constructing Coherence? Young Adults' Pursuit of Meaning through Multiple Transitions between Work, Education and Unemployment', *Journal of Youth Studies* 10, no. 2 (2007): 203–21.

[21] Kerry Young, *The Art of Youth Work*, 2nd edn (Lyme Regis: Russell House, 2006).

as 'What do you understand by this?' are asked. It is a practice where self-understanding is built and reshaped. It is also a practice within which God is disclosed and a new understanding of how God is present is realized. For Baker, testimony is not 'recital of a conversion experience' but 'honest talk about God's activity in the daily events of the here and now' and 'includes emerging stories that give meaning to one's life'.[22] Evoking testimony through guided conversation is one way that Baker suggests young people can be helped to realize God at work in their lives. Testimony helps to give the 'identity capital' young people need to express their faith identity. Sharing testimony in this way is also connected to young people's experiences of encounter in worship and prayer, which is the next core set of identity practices.

Encounter: mediation through participation

Another crucial set of practices involves the variety of interactive ways of praying that are part and parcel of many youth groups, including Impact and No. 1. The experience and sense of God gained in these activities – such as the 'rocks' prayer activity described by Phillip, the experience of prayer that Nicky discusses in Youth Alpha and the sense of God in large worship events – are all crucial elements of the spirituality of these young people.

Prayer is not an unsurprising practice to see at the heart of intentional Christian community; what is important in interactive, or multisensory, prayer, is the way in which it can facilitate encounter with God and engagement in conversation. We know from the work of Savage and others that prayer is adopted by Christian and non-Christian young people as a way of managing their life experiences – good and bad. However, in communal prayer there is a dimension to this handling of life experience that is helpfully outwardly focused – it is set in a clearer theological context. This context is also often talked about or taught about.

---

[22] Dori Grinenko Baker, *Doing Girlfriend Theology: God-Talk with Young Women* (Cleveland, OH: Pilgrim Press, 2005).

Prayer activities in Impact and No. 1 are usually structured around an area of Christian understanding: presenting God as someone who cares about our future, inviting the confession of sin or affirming the need for guidance. This is crucial for indwelling key understandings of tradition – something that Mark Yaconelli and others advocate in a recovery of contemplative prayer.[23] Yet it is also often structured to be highly participatory, involving movement, objects, drawing and symbolic acts such as writing, ripping up or placing prayers into God's hands. By making this participatory to express feeling, set fire to sins or problems, or tear up negative feelings, prayer is moved into the realm of identity work. In participatory prayer young people do things – not just say things – that help to express and connect the issue and identity conflicts they face in prayer. This connects to historic practices such as Communion as well as to freer types of prayer activities, although in the latter there is often more scope to discuss and reflect on what the meaning in the encounter was.

Participation is crucial to this sense of encounter. This is felt more broadly in larger gatherings, or during events, camps and pilgrimages. In these contexts the practices of worship and prayer may be no different from those in a home church, but they are highlighted by young people as more significant. It is difficult to replicate these on an ongoing basis, largely because a key attribute of these events is size. However, the use of songs from these events helps to generate the points of encounter young people require. Increasingly too the 'things' associated with these activities are important.[24] Several conversations with young people in Impact and No. 1 referenced the importance of having a worship album playing while on the bus, or proudly demonstrating the wristbands and T-shirts from such events. These things in a very tangible sense allow young people to carry around with them the memory – and continued point – of encounter. The more we can utilize

---

[23] Mark Yaconelli, *Contemplative Youth Ministry* (London: SPCK, 2006).

[24] Pete Ward, *Participation and Mediation: A Practical Theology for the Liquid Church* (London: SCM Press, 2008).

this approach in church-based worship, youth worship and participatory prayer, then the more 'means' we have to offer young people opportunities for encounter (see Figure 4).

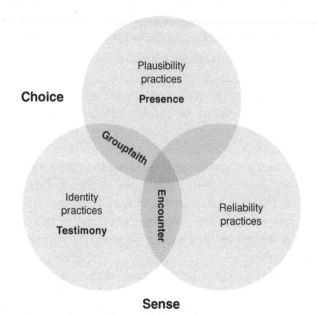

Figure 4 The importance of testimony and encounter to make sense of faith choices and God's existence

Reliability practices: making faith work in real life

In Chapter 4 the notion of 'use' highlighted the fact that young people need to find means of forming a reliable faith. In this exploration we noted that lifestyle practices embrace the sense that participation in the group ought to be part of forming and expressing faith identity and recognizing how reliance on the group is a key part of holding this identity. The dual function of the group in this sense is to be a place of reliability, but also a place where the reliability of the faith being formed is tested. This is seen through the practice of *attendance*, where young people invest significance in attending the group as a faith practice to help support their Christian lifestyle. This attendance is also key in developing a practice of *discernment*, where distinctive learning is given to seeking and interpreting what a Christian lifestyle should look like.

Attendance: youth groups as ritual

The appreciation of youth groups as a ritual comes from a comment made by Phillip about Impact, and is also seen in the way Mark talks about No. 1. The practice of attending the group is one that young people themselves see as important in their own faith – they need to get there and be there. When they are not, the youth leaders or other young people are active in finding out why, or working out how to help make it happen if other circumstances make this hard. In a very real sense this 'belonging as believing' is a vital practice to nurture. This is an area where organization and coordination of activities is paramount – and one of the key servant-leadership tasks that youth leaders and youth workers provide. It is not just 'going to the youth group' in this context. Attendance is one of the key issues identified in the exploration of factors around decline, and ways of providing alternative opportunities for young people are seen in the youth ministry responses. This, though, appears to be different. It is the rhythm that this offers which is cited as important as well as the benefit felt from being there. In many respects this is a 'born-again' practice; it is not a ritual in the same sense as taking Communion, but it is a ritual that has significance.

Another benefit of attendance that makes a difference for young people is the pastoral care that the group offers – the sense of connection to other people who know what they are going through. The young people in Impact and No. 1 feel conflict around their sense of Christian identity keenly. The continual requirement to choose requires a continual reference point and reference group for a choice to believe. Without this continual reminder not only does the plausibility of belief take a knock but the practice of faith too. It is within these groups that young people can express the emotions and feelings that arise from their own experience of faith. While leaders are mentioned as supportive in this – especially in missional contexts – it is in belonging to this larger group that identity conflict is lessened. Where parents continue to be a supportive factor in faith, the need to form and express an individual identity that builds from this base is also made possible by participation in a group. The sense of identity gained through participation in youth groups and youth events should not be underestimated, or seen as a precursor to believing. Young people's sense of belonging is a crucial part of believing, and youth ministry groups help to extend and expand this. The practice of attending, then, should be viewed as an element of faith generation, not a precursor (see Figure 5 on p. 144).

Discernment: interpreting and acting

The focus on experience and the reliance on the group do, however, require practices that enable young people to check this 'belonging as believing' in relation to how this is helping to facilitate encounter and transformation in God. In a similar vein to the development of theological thinking in groupfaith, the place of theological reflection is vital here – and also in relation to processing the sense of encounter.

The use of reflective learning cycles that invite reflection upon experience or action, explore and connect this to some aspect of Christian understanding, and aim towards a new understanding or revised action are a core aspect of the youth work practice that has become common in youth ministry.[25] As noted earlier, this approach is a feature of the informal education that underpins youth work activity – where young people are encouraged to move from 'dependence to independence' and to be able to 'reflect upon and take responsibility for their own actions'.[26] Programmes and curricula bought 'off the shelf' with 'ready to use' sessions frequently have this format. Helping young people to develop such skills may also be done by workers and leaders who themselves have been trained to reflect theologically. As youth groups meet frequently, the effect is that of a spiral – where processes of

[25] A classic book that expounds on this is Michael Warren, *Youth Gospel Liberation*, 3rd edn (Dublin: Veritas, 1998).

[26] John W. Ellis, 'Informal Education: A Christian Perspective', in *Using Informal Education: An Alternative to Casework, Teaching and Control?*, ed. Tony Jeffs and Mark Smith, Innovations in Education (Milton Keynes: Open University Press, 1990), 89–100.

theological reflection are repeated and understanding evolves. Youth ministry is perhaps one of the only areas of church life where this approach is so strongly structured. Culturally it is also perhaps the best context for this. It fits with the experience of school, it can be done often with irreverence and fun, and it is not as emotionally laden as discussing and questioning similar topics with parents.

This approach, however, can be taken further by stretching a reflection on a topic or issue into a deeper practice of discernment. David White argues that practices of discernment form the 'language of soul' and of 'Christian action'; they help shape the way in which we reflect on what God might be saying to us and asking us to do, on what we might be feeling and feeling the need to achieve. In seeking to foster practices of discernment, attention is given to ways of listening to our own emotions and to God's voice, remembering or reimagining God's presence and activity, and seeking to identify what to do next, calling to mind what God might say to us or want of us in our daily lives and vocation.[27]

Discernment practices are often the antithesis of the high-energy, fun elements we associate with youth ministry. However, they need not be unimaginative and can be highly interactive. What lies at the heart of discernment practices is a recovery of tradition and theology where young people are invited to explore and understand what is going on in the world around them, and in their world. It fosters habits of asking questions and making connections. This approach goes across the different activities in which young people might engage, but is particularly relevant when trying to unpick particular experiences, whether of God or life. It is also particularly apt for young people at a time in their lives when options and choices, or missed options and unsuccessful choices, mix with the experiences of disappointments and dilemmas in relationships. Again such activities lie at the heart of youth work practice, but in the context of faith generation can be deliberately set so that young people's sense of reliability in faith

---

[27] David F. White, *Practicing Discernment with Youth: A Transformative Youth Ministry Approach*, Youth Ministry Alternatives (Cleveland, OH: Pilgrim Press, 2005).

connects with their questions and options in vocation. In one session of Impact, for instance, the question posed was to think through what effect the young people wanted to have on and in the world and to discuss how this connected to their faith (or how it didn't). In No. 1 the key role of discipler often encompassed giving advice on careers and school subject options. While care is of course needed here, this again is a connection supported by a mature and trained leader, or a group trained to be peer mentors.

In practising discernment a core aspect is to allow young people to explore the complexity of the issues they are drawn to, not to seek simple solutions. It is also crucial to have clear ways in which connection to the Christian tradition and story can be made. This is often helpfully done in programmed activities where these can be drawn out, but can also be part and parcel of the ordinary theology of group conversation. In this way, experience can lead into explorations that raise questions about the nature of the world as well as the nature of God. Discernment through

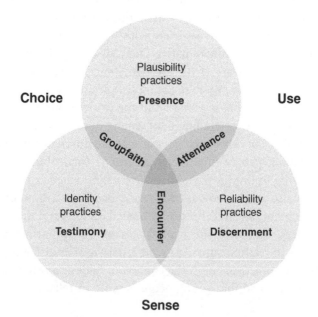

Figure 5 The reliability practices of attendance and discernment in learning to 'use' faith and extend plausibility

exploration also involves coming to a form of judgement or decision. Here the identification of questions such as 'What do you think God is saying?' or 'So what should we do about this as a group?' is a key element of making discernment part of the task of youth groups as intentional Christian community (see Figure 5).

In discernment and vocation there is also a strong emphasis on externalizing what might otherwise be internalized experiences. Such a focus is vitally important because in faith generation we have sets of practices that are also specifically set to affirm and enable meeting with God in worship or being free and more at ease in allowing a guard down in conversation with Christian friends. Discernment and vocation can help to explore where God might be found elsewhere in our lives and also help to push our sense of plausibility to the places where we go to school or work.

Faith generation: patterns and practices for growth

These patterns and practices are the basis for youth ministry as faith generation. They are the responses that need to be put in place to tackle the reality of generational decline, and the limited outcomes of mission work. One cannot assume that putting these in place will inevitably lead to success, but tracing the connection between these patterns and practices and the challenges of choice, sense and use would strongly suggest their efficacy. Here, Voas' analogy of the decline in faith as analogous to radioactive decay is a helpful metaphor.

Voas describes the Church having a half-life of one generation, since every generation loses 50 per cent of its believers. While this decline, like radioactive decay, appears uniform on a graph, it is in fact a random process. There is no predictive theory available to say which atoms will decay and which will remain. The place of faith in young people's lives, the circumstances in which they live this out and the influences on each young person's faith formation are similarly complex. While affirming that faith is both gift and work it is true that some do not choose to receive this gift – whether we interpret this through the impact of sin, as Bass considers this, or the lack of plausibility as MacLaren has it. We

Table 1 The pattern and practices of faith generation: a summary

Plausibility practices		
Challenge addressed	*Example practices*	*Capacity generated*
Choice The need to choose to believe in a secular age and the implausibility of doing so	**Presence:** takes the youth ministry practice of making spaces for young people and resets this as one of building 'places to be Christian'	As plausibility shelters, youth groups offer places where the task of trying to be Christian is enabled. They also contribute to rebuilding our ecology for faith formation
The continuing requirement to choose to hold to faith and the impact this has on identity	**Groupfaith:** takes the youth ministry approaches of intentional relationships and distinct learning and applies these to address the challenge of choice as collaborative catechesis	Ordinary and ordered learning helps 'affirm' faith in the face of challenge and scepticism and create new ways of imagining possible faith
Identity practices		
Challenge addressed	*Example practices*	*Capacity generated*
Sense The need to experience God, to sense God's presence in concrete encounters	**Testimony:** forms a structured practice that enables young people to own and understand experience of God and to make meaning from experiences	Enables young people to develop a coherent understanding of their Christian identity and to root this in experiences and memories

Challenge addressed	Example practices	Capacity generated
The continuing requirement to make sense of faith in a secular context – an intellectually secure and emotionally resonant faith	**Encounter:** makes the multisensory and interactive transformational practices common in youth ministry central to prayer and worship in large and small events	Gives opportunities to experience transcendence and develop a readiness to seek and identify God's ongoing activity

Reliability practices

Challenge addressed	Example practices	Capacity generated
Use The need for faith to be a reliable source of identity and agency – the way in which we are empowered to face and act in the world	**Attendance:** 'coming to the youth group' and attending 'youth events' become two markers that help form a Christian lifestyle	Makes participation in a youth group a way of giving a sense of agency in personal faith
The continuing need to connect and relate all aspects of life to faith and not segment or partition what is seen as sacred	**Discernment:** makes central the need to test and learn from others and tradition in order to make wise faith decisions	Helps to balance how meaning making and agency are not given over to 'self-help' but to a broader sense of self-understanding and vocation

cannot predict whether our actions will cause faith to be gained, or lost, for particular young people. We can pray that it is gained and grows. At the same time we can put in place the pattern and practices of faith generation in youth ministry to act both as an inhibitor to the general decline in faith and as an accelerant for growth.

The patterns and practices of faith generation are built on the premise that the transmission of faith requires us to address the specific challenges to faith formation in a secular age (summarized in Table 1). This approach, however, goes further than some strands of thinking which assert that we somehow simply need to help young people 'stick' with church or faith. The real challenge is to help young people generate faith that can thrive in a secular age. This includes the ongoing resilience to choose to believe and to grow in confidence, with the opportunity to make sense of faith. It also involves the challenge of building a faith where God is not treated as an imaginary friend with whom we can share our problems, but as a reliable presence in our world, personally encountered. Faith generation addresses the challenges of forming faith in a secular age and builds the capacity to continue to do so. Both aspects are required.

This is the urgent task I began with as the primary challenge the Church faces. In the next chapter I will outline how the impact of this focus is not only applicable to the specific issue of the failure in faith transmission, but is also a key for growth in other ways. This I hope will press the case even further that it is this area of pastoral mission that should be prioritized.

Questions for discussion

1 Thinking about the patterns of practice that faith generation illustrates, what is your response to the need to move from faith development to generation, to embrace the construction of identity and to see youth ministry groups as intentional Christian communities?

2 If you are a youth leader or worker, analyse the three spheres of practices. Which of these are present in your youth ministry context and what other activities might fit into these areas?

3 Thinking about young people you know, which of the practices mentioned do you think might be most formative in helping them to form faith?

4 If you wanted to take forward this model, where would you start?

7

Faith generation and church growth

————•·•·•————

*Youth Ministry's great potential may lie in its ability to
re-imagine the church on behalf of the wider Christian
community, a church in which God has called young
people to play an irrepressible and irreplaceable part.*
                                        (Root and Dean[1])

Without intentional work to stem generational decline the Church
will not be in a position to grow. The passing on of faith from
one generation to the next is no longer a 'natural' phenomenon.
It does not happen any more through general processes of socialization or enculturation. In fact, the pressures against faith being
passed on are more likely to prevail. As a result, church communities – parents, leaders, young people and members – need to be
organized and intentional in faith generation.

The research findings suggesting that a children's or youth minister is the most valuable lay role a church can appoint if it is to
grow are not coincidental, but church growth is also not solely
down to that one individual! It works if this person is helping to
support and sustain an intentional Christian community through
which young people can actively engage in shaping and expressing
their faith identity. It works if this person has a team that he or
she can join with in this task. It works if this person and that team
are also engaged in knitting this work into the life of the community of faith of which they are a part. In seeking strategies to
promote growth it might seem like a chicken-and-egg question
as to whether a focus on children and young people promotes

---

[1] Andrew Root and Kenda Creasy Dean, *The Theological Turn in Youth Ministry* (Downer's
Grove, IL: IVP, 2011), 35.

growth, or whether this focus comes when a church is growing. It is also true that the *From Anecdote to Evidence* research affirms that there is 'no single recipe for growth'. However, by underscoring the need for faith generation I am arguing that this is at the very least a necessary baking ingredient, not the icing on the cake.

In this final chapter I will assess how to frame the theology of practice outlined in Chapter 6 as part of a holistic strategy for growth. This places faith generation in a central position, not only for stemming further decline, but also for stimulating growth beyond this. Faith generation focused on work with children and young people contributes to the wider vitality of a church community. To help illustrate this I will look at three imaginary examples where a deliberate strategy of faith generation is required: St Hilda's, Barnabas Christian Fellowship (BCF) and the gAp project. I use these three projects (based in the same imaginary town) to represent some model types of churches in the current context in the UK. St Hilda's is what might be described as a church with a 'low base'; it is not atypical of churches across the UK in having only a handful of young people. Here the challenge is starting any real youth work at all! Barnabas Christian Fellowship is a church on the threshold of growth. It is in the zone that CPAS, an Anglican evangelical mission agency working with churches in the UK and Republic of Ireland, identifies as on the brink of becoming a 'large church'. This positions BCF at a decision point of having to adapt its communal life to grow beyond an adult congregation size of 120. Here the challenge is in adapting the youth provision in the church to be a contributive factor in its growth. Finally, in the gAp project I have retained a focus on a direct mission project and how this can factor in the faith generation strategy for the town where St Hilda's and BCF are located. (Note: any similarity to churches of a similar name is entirely coincidental!)

I will begin, though, by looking at how a faith generation approach to youth ministry is a vital contribution to a growing church, in what it can add to the wider life and ministry of these communities of faith. In relation to this I will also briefly highlight how decline in young people is not just a numerical issue for the Church of the future, but a tragic loss of active members of God's

Church today. To demonstrate this I will illustrate how young people's disruptive presence can be a provocation for godly growth. There is a strong tradition in youth ministry of championing young people as being the Church of today, not the Church of tomorrow. If we are to achieve ambitions to 'grow younger' and enable young people and young adults to form and express faith, we have to be prepared to not only make the structural and theological changes for faith generation, but also enable these generations to take a fuller part in the faith life of our churches and congregations. Where churches engage in intentional faith generation this can be fostered so that young people's contributions to church life might be received as a gift to steer us towards new ways of being churches that grow in depth as well as size.

Growing Christian presence: the 'vitality' contribution of children and youth work

When the Church acts towards faith generation, it is engaged in evolving patterns and practices that meet the 'new challenges and conditions' in the context where Christian presence is being sought.[2] In faith generation the Church can respond to the conditions of faith that we all now live in, not only young people. The impact of holding faith in a secular age is felt at the fault line of the transmission of faith between generations, but we all live out our faith in this context. As such, many of the patterns and practices in youth ministry are the approaches to, and understanding of, faith that will help the Church be more prescient and prophetic within this broader culture.

Pete Ward discusses how many of the approaches to fellowship, worship and Christian events that are seen across the Church – certainly in the evangelical churches – have their origins in youth ministry.[3] The expressions of faith that are observed in events like

---

[2] James W. Fowler, 'The Emerging New Shape of Practical Theology', in *Practical Theology: International Perspectives*, ed. Friedrich Schweitzer and Johannes A. van der Ven, Erfahrung und Theologie, Bd 340172-1135 (Frankfurt am Main/New York: P. Lang, 1999), 75–92 (83).
[3] Pete Ward, *Growing up Evangelical: Youthwork and the Making of a Subculture* (London: SPCK, 1996).

World Youth Day in the Roman Catholic Church display a similar phenomenon. In part this is because these types of activities are an extension of the plausibility practices that are a core aspect of faith generation. The same is perhaps also true of the Fresh Expressions movement. Not only does this area of church life retain a strong theme of seeking ways to connect with younger people, but also many of those involved in these projects have a significant previous history in youth work or ministry. If one were to analyse these types of contexts I would expect that a similar pattern of faith generation would be present. Similarly the increase in young adults in cathedral congregations merits attention in this regard,[4] as does the re-engagement in small local community churches that is beginning to be seen in the US context.[5] Activity that begins to address the challenge of the intergenerational transmission of faith has a history of drift into the mainstream life of the Church. We learn things about the emerging context by engaging with this context as it emerges.

This contribution to the evolution of church practice is important, but it is also the case that the plausibility practices put in place for faith generation in youth ministry have a direct contribution to those needed by the church community as a whole, particularly for churches that are seeking to grow. I have argued that the practices we need to adopt must directly address the challenges of faith in a secular age. It is highly likely that such approaches would also be beneficial for those who connect to churches from a limited or non-faith background. Churches that have adopted a faith generation approach in their children and youth ministry are more likely to be able to adopt a similar approach in their welcome and nurture of adults, whether this is in running and using Alpha, being more interactive in prayer and worship styles, or seeing discipleship not as a process of osmosis but as a task that requires intentional activity. This intentional focus on faith generation among children and young people can

---

[4] *From Anecdote to Evidence: Findings from the Church Growth Research Programme 2011–13* (London: The Church of England, 2014), 23.

[5] Naomi Schaefer Riley, *Got Religion? How Churches, Mosques, and Synagogues Can Bring Young People Back* (West Conshohocken, PA: Templeton Press, 2014), 17–34.

help to enable presence and contribute towards the plausibility practices required for faith to flourish in a secular age.

A focus on faith generation requires rebuilding the ecology of faith in a local area. Simply put, activities with children and young people can extend Christian presence in an area better than many other options. If a church is able to extend its presence to work through local schools, this helps relocate or reinforce the church's role as a part of a local community. If it is able to organize a Sunday school or Sunday group for children and young people and advertise this to families enquiring for baptism, or offer the use of the church hall for a party, this extends presence beyond the children and young people who might be involved. An intentional focus on faith generation helps this to be Christian presence, not only social presence, as the activities are focused on this outcome and engagement begins from this point. Family services, too, become important points of contact for these extended networks; when done well, these can provide and maintain a main point of contact for the parents, grandparents and carers of kids involved in church activities. Events that are primarily for adults are unlikely to lead to this web of family connections being established. This is especially important for missional projects, not only as a mark of good practice, but also as a way of authentically connecting to wider family networks. Some projects, such as KidzClubs and SuperKids, try to ensure that this is undertaken as a core part of the leaders' task – visiting homes to take information and make contact.

A focus on faith generation requires a community response to the challenges and responses to faith in a secular age. Where there are activities that children and young people find encouraging and enjoyable, this has a direct impact on adults who come to the church. Parenting in the faith is a challenge; parents are the first to notice and have to engage with the challenges faced by their children and young people in holding faith in a secular age. As I will discuss in the next section, a challenge that remains under-emphasized in faith generation is to find better ways to support parents in this task. However, if a church is providing intentional activities to children and young people then there is arguably the potential to provide more effective ministry to adults as well. Adults are perhaps more likely to participate in additional events because they have confidence in the church's provision and are potentially more likely to be positive about their participation to others at their life stage – because they know that this church is helping to meet the needs that they have with their children. Similarly, adults with families who connect to the church as a consequence of their own spiritual journey are more likely to be able to connect to that community if they can do so through bringing their children to events, or knowing that these are available. This is not to downplay concerns over churches being family focused to the exclusion of those who do not have, or do not want, children. However, what it stresses is that a focus on developing provision for children and young people has extensive benefits beyond the immediate focus of the kids themselves. It helps nurture vitality.

Enabling Christian presence: the disruptive growth influence of children and young people

In a thin but provocative book, *Like Dew Your Youth*, the biblical scholar Eugene Peterson talks about the role that young people can play in renewing faith within families, churches and congregations.[6] Peterson sees the time of adolescence as mainly disruptive – which can be received either positively or negatively! Receiving this disruption as unwelcome but necessary for growth is the stance he sees as biblically rooted. Others, such as David White, whom I quoted earlier, go further, highlighting the fact that young people and young adults are often 'domesticated' by adults; they are pushed into a holding category of 'adolescent' until they become 'adult'. White stresses that with the hindsight of history this may well be a mistake, highlighting the significant roles teenagers and young adults have held in previous generations.[7] Young people, he

---

[6] Eugene H. Peterson, *Like Dew Your Youth: Growing Up with Your Teenager* (Grand Rapids, MI: Eerdmans, 1994).

[7] David F. White, *Practicing Discernment with Youth: A Transformative Youth Ministry Approach*, Youth Ministry Alternatives (Cleveland, OH: Pilgrim Press, 2005), 16.

suggests, are a *charism* – a gift to the Church – contributing 'beauty, energy, critical challenge, passion, compassion, curiosity, camaraderie' and more besides.[8] Growing churches, I believe, grow in part because they respond to this disruption and receive this gift, whether this is from young people who have grown up in their midst or young people they have sought to connect with in their community.

The first area we might consider is the way in which young people move from being 'learners' to 'deciders'. The key issue at the heart of decline we have identified is that almost half of our young people are deciding to leave the Church. Peterson sees the movement from being learners to being deciders as the crucial change that Christian parents struggle with. This correlates with the issue of choice discussed earlier. If, in moving from learners to deciders, young people are deciding to leave, then as a Church we perhaps have something to learn! In this book I have focused on a theology of practice that might aid the transmission of faith from one generation to the next. Where this is breaking down, intentional action is required. However, where it is being successfully accomplished, there are things to learn. That has been the basis of the case studies I have drawn on in Chapters 3, 4 and 5.

The evidence that parents are reticent in making it a priority to pass on their faith, as highlighted by the *From Anecdote to Evidence* research, is likely to be an indication that parents do not see the need, or do not know how, to attempt the intentional activities required for faith generation. In this regard a clear focus on the task of faith generation among young people calls all in the community of faith to the task of establishing Christian presence. Arguments for the centrality of the family in passing on faith are correct; faith generation does not undercut this, but rather augments it to help highlight the types of practices that all Christians in a secular age need to be aware of and engaged in. In this the idea of faith transmission as moving one way – from older to younger generations – is turned on its head. The transmission of faith should always be a multidirectional process. Churches that

---

[8] White, *Practicing Discernment*, 16.

learn from young people about how they engage in faith generation are perhaps more likely to be the types of churches that provide the same sort of environments for the increasing number of 'nones', that is, people who identify as having no religion. If we want to engage in mission and pastoral work to 'nones', it will be our young people and young adults who should be able to tell us the basics of this, as they are the people who have learnt to form faith for a secular age.

The second thing we need to learn is how to better receive young people as our co-learners in Christ. Peterson again sees this as a disruptive reminder to parents and the community of faith: if we want to grow, then we need to experience and receive disruption. Growth requires being able to accommodate growth, and where young people are growing up (in Christ) the disruption that comes with this can help to set these conditions. One of the myths that adults might tell themselves in their middle age is that they have no more growing up to do – nothing new to learn. Peterson says this about such a challenge:

> In a world where differences frequently degenerate into conflicts, the parent generation must take the lead in showing that generational differences are opportunities for an exchange of personal love, faith, and hope – not occasions to seek an advantage or assert a superiority.[9]

In faith generation I have described a key process as the 'indwelling and construction of faith', a task that is new for every generation. As such, a young person or young adult's faith should not look like that of their parents. There should be a family resemblance but it should look different! This difference can be rightly provocative towards growth in the depth of our own faith.

This challenge relates to the movement from being a 'Christian parent' to being a 'Christian person' as the nature of relating to young adult family members changes. There is of course much more to say on this, but this is not a book on parenting. What this entails for adults is a significant shift in their own identity

---

[9] Peterson, *Like Dew Your Youth*, 45.

and sense of self. I remember running a parenting course for a church and talking about the scene in the movie *Mamma Mia* where the lead character sings 'Slipping Through My Fingers' as she reflects on her daughter growing up and moving on. Tears flowed, and not just among the mums in the room! Effective pastoral care of young people through this time is a contributive factor to the effective pastoral care of adult members. If this time period is met with security and support then this can be a generative time for all. This is not only about personal fulfilment and growth; it is also about investing in the people who, once their parental responsibilities have lessened, will themselves be more attuned as mature Christians able to lead areas of ministry, or extend their personal task of establishing Christian presence in their own vocations.

Intentional action to promote faith generation attends to the task of growth by providing the conditions in which both numerical growth and growth in depth can occur. First and foremost this is required to counter the current decline in young people's continued participation in church. However, this focus, more than many other initiatives, also contributes to the broader connections churches require in the task of growing Christian presence. In addition, faith generation is a crucial aspect to set the conditions of growth for all believers. It sets out a clear direction that faith does require fresh expression, and all can freshly express that faith. In the final sections of this chapter I will summarize how the imaginary churches, St Hilda's and BCF, can begin to address this challenge.

Building from a low base: fostering faith generation where it is needed most

Churches like St Hilda's, with a low base from which to build faith generation, face two distinct challenges. The first is how they can best attend to the needs for faith generation with the children and young people they have in their midst. The second is how they might be able to build from a focus on this pressing 'internal' need to one that begins to engage in the task of extending Christian presence in their community. Such a church might respond in one of the following ways.

Nurture and network

With only a few young people, St Hilda's faces a critical challenge in being able to form a group of sufficient size to make an impact in the plausibility practices that undergird faith generation. One approach requires the recognition that they do not have enough young people to make faith generation plausible. What they can do is to seize the opportunity to form a small group for the young people that they do have, an intentional group through which a programme of discussion-based teaching could be run. This opens up the possibility of connecting this group with a larger youth group in the area, or with several other small groups from churches of a similar size. At the same time, St Hilda's could focus on providing sufficient activities for younger children in the know-ledge that there will be some level of provision for these kids when they are older.

The benefits of this approach are that they would be able to run such activities with the small volunteer base. If the members of St Hilda's were fortunate they might even be able to borrow time from a gap-year volunteer from a Christian organization or other church. The small group running at St Hilda's could do so using published curriculum material – such as *Roots: Children & Young People*[10] or Youth for Christ's *Mettle*.[11] If this small group met midweek then the young people would be able to participate in Sunday services and could even be given roles of responsibility within this; perhaps if they felt able, this could include helping with the activities for younger children. This different type of engagement, as we saw in the case studies, can often provoke a sense of participation in church as intentional community.

By networking with other churches, young people from St Hilda's can link their young people with other young Christians for joint social and worship events. In so doing these churches would be

---

[10] See <www.rootsontheweb.com>.
[11] See <www.yfcresources.co.uk/mettle-home>.

able to provide the plausibility and generative practices associated with faith generation. This network might also open up the opportunity for the groups to attend larger worship events if these are running in the area, or enjoy time away at a Christian festival or youth camp. This approach requires trust and cooperation between churches in the local area or denominational grouping. In the latter example the denomination may be able to organize the connections to larger worship events, camps, festivals and youth pilgrimages. In many rural contexts this approach is perhaps one of the only options available. As stressed in the discussion throughout the book, the most important aspect of faith generation is appreciating that intentional action is required. St Hilda's is not in a position to fulfil all of the elements of the theology of practice for faith generation I have outlined. However, with other churches together, they are.

Merge and re-curve

This approach is similar to that of 'nurture and network', but is slightly more radical in that it involves a decision around the identity and direction of the whole church community. In this scenario St Hilda's would choose to merge all of the activities for young people with those of another church, assuming there is a church with the resources to run a youth ministry capable of investing in patterns and practices of faith generation. This option might be chosen because on closer inspection it does not seem that there is the capacity for a small group, or the leaders to help resource it and manage the network connections. Merging would be a brave decision as it would be highly likely that if young people from St Hilda's became part of another church's youth group they might very well end up joining that church if they stayed in the area.

In this approach it is possible that new families may still join the church community, and St Hilda's could focus on providing some activities for children. By promoting the link to the youth work in the partner church, this would help to communicate that the members of St Hilda's are actively interested in and resourcing work with young people. It should communicate enough that parents with younger children could have confidence that this church is interested in ministering to all ages. Further, this leaves St Hilda's with the potential to focus on other areas of ministry and mission within its community. For instance, church members could seek to engage students in their area by offering hospitality to this age group. They could focus on hosting more community activities if they have the premises. They would also continue to be a worshipping community praying for and nurturing these links. While engaging in this active, growth-focused, mission, they can reconsider their approach to children and young people, particularly if these new approaches begin to regenerate family contacts and links.

Sow and start again

It may be that St Hilda's have only a couple of young people, but happen to have a thriving toddlers' playgroup which uses their building and connects the church to a number of local families. Here, then, the deliberate decision might be to focus energies on building children's and family work from this starting point, adopting an understanding that faith generation patterns and practices will have to be part of the long-term planning for this vision. The young people they do have could be connected to another church youth group, or there could simply be a more concerted effort to draw them in to the main life of the congregation as best they can. This approach would at least still give the possibility of young people having a greater investment in the intentional activity of enabling Christian presence within the whole community of faith, particularly if this were genuinely supported. The weakness would be that this approach lacks the plausibility practices and reliability practices that come with the social–faith contact with peers.

Given that St Hilda's has connections with younger children, this could be the beginning of a new strategy for faith generation, starting with this younger group and offering the possibility for the young people to become leaders and helpers in it. While I have not focused on the shape of this practice among children and families, it should be very similar in principle to the spheres of practice I have outlined. This choice is one that still requires intentional action, but a key difference here is that this activity will have a whole family focus as well as specific activities for children.

What is also important in this approach is to be aware of the 'next phase requirements' as children grow older. If this approach works well, St Hilda's will have to determine if the cohort of children they have might form a reasonably sized youth group. It is likely that St Hilda's may still need to consider one of the options of partnering with other churches to develop a network group that could serve St Hilda's and other churches in their area.

Growing from a firm base: embracing faith generation as a key to growth in numbers and depth

Churches at the threshold of growth have an increased require-ment for attending to the task of faith generation as they have a greater number of children and young people in their midst. They are also at the point where a viable strategy for growing this area of mission and ministry can be better resourced. However, they are also vulnerable to the 'natural development' paradigm of faith formation and as such need to consider how the patterns and practices of faith generation can be put in place. This is the challenge for Barnabas Christian Fellowship.

Consolidate and connect

Barnabas Christian Fellowship has a group of young people and a small team of volunteers who have been running the activities with them for a couple of years. They also run a couple of groups for younger children on a Sunday. The key task for BCF is to consolidate their provision so that the work they do with young people is ready for these younger children as they move through and fit for purpose with the group they already have. As a church, BCF is also at a pivotal point in its size. They have already employed a half-time administrator and are considering taking on an assist-ant minister or a youth worker. In expanding their staff team, BCF are at a key change point in how they organize the life of the church. It is important, then, at this phase to be very clear about the role that they would want an employed person to undertake.

One option is to find the person who can take the key coordinator role for work with children and young people. This will involve direct work with the age group with which he or she is most comfortable or experienced, but also attention to growing and sustaining the volunteer team.

The task of connecting children and youth ministry together involves consolidating the different groups that the church runs. A problem BCF has is that it does not have a building that can be used during the week. The newly appointed children and youth worker has identified that the majority of children and young people within the church are between the ages of 10 and 14. There are a handful of older young people and some younger children as well. In consultation with the parents the youth worker has proposed setting up a new group for 10-to-14-year-olds that will meet on a Friday night for a youth club in a church hall they are renting. The worker would coordinate the team of volunteers in running this club. Some of the older young people will help as volunteers in their own small groups, one for boys and one for girls. These will be peer-led and the youth worker will meet with leaders and perhaps support each young person in turn in the opportunity to lead these groups. On a Sunday the main focus for children's activities will be for the younger children and the 10-to-14s. The older young people will stay on in the main service, with a couple of them playing in the worship band. As well as connecting together work across the age groups, another connecting task the youth worker wishes to do is to find what other events there are in the area that the older young people could participate in.

This approach helps to put in place as much of the three sets of practices as can be achieved by BCF at this point. While it is focused on the young people that they already have, it is not inward-looking inasmuch as a key value the worker wants to instigate is to be welcoming towards the young people's friends, especially at the Friday night group but also on a Sunday morning. The small groups for the older young people are designed to be just for them, and as well as having a discussion series that they follow are mainly for sharing and prayer. The worker has also arranged to take the older young people to a Christian festival in the summer.

Open up and adjust

A second approach that BCF could consider is to focus activities on opening up their youth work to the housing estate close to the school where the young people meet. Several of the church members are keen to be more outward-looking and suggest that in employing a youth worker they might be able to achieve this. However, in opening up their youth work, care has to be taken not to confuse the priorities of the process of faith generation.

The worker has a small team of volunteers and between them arranges to help run three sessions within the week. These could include two small groups for 11–14s, one for boys and one for girls, that will meet midweek at one of the young people's homes, led by the volunteers. They will also run Sunday groups for the under-8-to-11s and those aged over 11. Work with the young kids will also continue, but the worker isn't responsible for this. This team will also help to put on a kids' club in the local school where they meet on a Friday night. The head teacher is keen to have the church run this and a couple of the parents from the school are also interested in helping. The kids' club is aimed at Year 6 pupils (10–11 years old) but is open to children aged up to 12. A couple of the church kids are in the school and are keen to come along.

The church has explained that the kids' club isn't just for church young people, but will be run using material from a Christian youth charity. This material involves lots of games and activities, but also has some elements that get young people to think about their lives and to reflect on some values and principles that come from Christian belief. The team has also decided to use the same organization's material for their church-based group. This costs a monthly fee, but has connected them to some other people in the area who also run these programmes.

This approach is a complex one. It involves working from two starting points that might meet in the middle. The church – as it seeks to grow – is helping to build links into the community where it meets and is directly engaging a, largely, new group of young people. The activities that they put on have a 'Christian flavour' and do encourage the young people to explore faith and spirituality through meaning-making practices, but how intentional this group can be and how robust the plausibility and generative practices are is more difficult to assess and will depend on the freedom they have to own this identity in working with the school. With their church groups there is a desire to enable the young people to deepen their understanding of and reflection on faith, and the small groups will help to provide an environment for this. However, there are some weaknesses in the plausibility practices that arise from not having a distinct place or a larger number of young people. A key challenge in the future is how these different spheres of work might cross over and connect. One option that the team could explore is whether the other leaders in the local area who run the same activity group might be interested in organizing a youth worship event, primarily for the church young people but also for members of the open groups if they were interested.

These approaches are not exhaustive; there are other options that BCF could take. What I illustrate here is again the mark of intentionality needed to ensure that attention is given to faith generation. The three spheres of activity I have outlined are helpful markers for reflecting on the nature of the provision that is planned or undertaken – asking what it might be helping to achieve. In seeking to engage young people not yet in the church – or at least on the fringes – I have highlighted the fact that this approach requires additional thought and action. Starting in the meaning-making sphere is a task that Christian youth work can undertake quite well. The key question for faith generation is whether this can be augmented to include plausibility and generative practices. With respect to Christian presence both approaches do help BCF to extend this. In the first approach they become more visible in the Friday night project and perhaps offer greater opportunity for friends of the young people to connect. In the second approach there is a clearer widening of networks to link with the school, which might have a more overt impact on the church through its becoming involved in other areas of activity with the school or on the estate. While BCF is not facing any challenge in shrinking, these illustrations also emphasize that whatever size a church is, the task of faith generation is one that needs active management. How a church responds to taking the challenge of faith generation forward will depend on the wider context in which it is situated.

Establishing a base for mission: furthering faith generation beyond the walls of the church

In the need to focus on the task for faith generation it is imperative that this pastoral need is not disconnected from the missional task of engaging young people away from the local church. A key aspect of Faith Identity Work highlighted in the case studies is that the challenges that young people raised in church contexts have in negotiating indwelling and constructing faith identity are different from those of their peers who might connect with faith at some stage. In the examples above I have kept this requirement in mind and suggested how the different strategies have both pastoral and missional benefits. In this section, however, I want to focus on approaches that are specifically geared around developing intentional communities where the majority of young people are from non-church backgrounds.

The gAp project

Members of BCF are keen to connect with the young people from their local area and recognize that in order to do so they will need a different approach from that used in the work they are doing with their young people. Rather than taking on an employed youth worker to work with the church young people, the church is keen to put these resources towards setting up a youth project on the housing estate near where they meet. They are clear that they want this to be a place where young people can encounter faith, but understand that this has to be given time to develop.

The BCF members approach the other churches in their area with the idea of starting a drop-in and agree to form a working group to look into this. This group identifies a potential venue in a community hall that has an annex that is underused. The group also gets in touch with the leaders of several other projects that appear to be running a similar type of venue. BCF agrees to put the money it has for a half-time worker into this project, which the working group decides should be run as a project of the local Churches Together group. Together the local churches fundraise to provide resources to start the drop-in. It takes time to find the right worker, but the drop-in looks like it is finally coming together. The worker focuses in the first six months of her time on going round to the local churches explaining what the gAp project is and what it is trying to achieve. Part of this work is to recruit helpers and volunteers. At the same time, she meets with local youth workers in the area and begins to see how the gAp fits into this scene. Through this networking she discovers that there is a grant available for some IT equipment and a training course she can go on to host a 'computer driving licence' course. As well as fitting out the kitchen to act as a small coffee bar, the team set aside one corner of the drop-in as a 'reflection space'. One option in this prayer space is to set up a box for prayers, with the promise that anything put in will be prayed for by the team. After a year of preparation the gAp project opens its doors . . .

The thumbnail sketch above outlines how the gAp is set up and illustrates again how intentional focus on our three spheres of faith generation is important. The first step involves making a neutral space into a Christian place. This is crucial in that the drop-in needs to be a place of plausibility but also open and accessible. Christian youth work done well in these contexts can engage in activities that focus on meaning making and empowerment, undertaken by drawing on Christian tradition and symbols. Again, if this is open and identifiable as an aspect of the venue's basis, then the connection of this project to Christianity is clearer. However, in doing this there has to be an identifiable benefit that is understandable in a more general sense: it may be that the project is aiming to support young people in developing life skills or IT skills; it may be that a focus on music or media is possible; or sports. There is the possibility here to connect with the interests of particular young people. If this is to be youth work provision it has to provide youth work provision.

Lastly, there has to be the capacity to include or connect to generative practices. Some groups have an associated worship event that happens away from the main drop-in. Here again the focus is for young people to express their connection points and journey towards an experience and understanding of God in conversation with the workers and volunteers in the project. In this type of project the intentionality of faith generation needs to be held very clearly by the group leading the project, as the tensions of working with these multiple focuses can often lead to this intention being weakened or to people just assuming that it will be happening!

The gAp church

An alternative approach that can be taken in creating a new missional base responds to the need for more overt plausibility and generative practices to be at the heart of faith generation – and also to the crisis in faith generation elsewhere within the Church. For a number of years there has been debate over the role that youth congregations or youth churches can play in supporting young people's faith. There are different types of models for these congregations. Most are of the type that involves monthly or less frequent worship events such as I have described earlier – put on by either an organization or a larger church. Some exist as evening congregations in larger churches, where there is a critical mass of young adults and young people – often in cities. There are a few, but only a few, long-standing congregations of this sort and where they are present there are strong arguments that they help to provide the three spheres of practices identified as essential for faith generation.[12] There are fewer examples of such models that are primarily missional, but this is another option for St Hilda's.[13]

St Hilda's is a large church, in that it has a large building. While there are a few younger children and a couple of teenagers

---

[12] Graham Cray, *Youth Congregations and the Emerging Church*, Grove Evangelism Series (Cambridge: Grove, 2002).

[13] Chris Russell, 'A Church for the Unchurched', in *Church Unlimited: Youthwork and Mission Today*, ed. Nicholas Shepherd and Jonathan Brant (Leicester: Youthwork the Partnership/Matador, 2008), 33–43.

connected to the church, the prospects for developing this area of church life are limited. Their vicar is also heading towards retirement and it is difficult to see how to make any changes that will enable St Hilda's to grow younger – as the diocese is asking them to do! In discussing the options for the future with clergy colleagues the vicar has learnt about a church in another town that has refocused its mission on becoming a church for non-church young people. After visiting this church it seems that this vision, and challenge, is a little beyond what St Hilda's can offer. However, in discussion with the church committee the vicar has approached the diocese to see if they can host or develop some sort of expression of church that might emulate this vision. In response to this the diocese agrees to keep funding for the clergy post in place, seeking to appoint someone with the skills and interests needed to pioneer this new phase for St Hilda's. The idea for the gAp church is born.

At first the idea was that St Hilda's would seek to shape its life around connecting with young people in the area and drawing a community of people together who wanted to participate in this task. This approach has been moderately successful, as they might have liked, but they have a group of people which is committed to helping fund and care for the building as the new vicar goes about the task of putting together a team of young adults that will work with him around a series of events and activities for young people in the area. The team put on a mixture of youth work activities, low-key prayer and worship services, as well as a regular Sunday service. One of the young people in the groups has asked if a team member could be her mentor, as her school has started a project to link Year 10 pupils (aged 14–15) with adults in business and the community. The volunteer agrees and also points out to the school that there are several other people in St Hilda's congregation who might be able to go through the vetting and training for this programme.

To their surprise some of the young people pitch up to all of these, although most come in and out of the youth work. In preparing for the project the pews have been removed in St Hilda's, with a few being taken down to the crypt which is now a chapel. Worship and prayer activities take place in different spaces, and during the youth work times the chapel area is often used for group discussions. One of the projects the young people are undertaking at the moment is to decorate the walls of the church with two murals: one that shows St Hilda's history, and one that depicts what they think and feel about life in their town. The hope is that these will be finished in time for the baptism and confirmation service planned for later in the year, at which five young people have said they are interested in being baptized . . .

As the gap between young people and the Church widens – in the sense that the starting point for exploring and understanding spirituality and faith is more rooted in that of a secular age – the need for places where young people can reconnect with the Christian tradition is vital. The drop-in-style project does this in one way, the gAp church in another. In both of these strategies there is recognition that faith generation requires a broader structural base that is connected to at least one church community, to help provide the conditions for nurture and growth in faith. Each of these examples might very well be considered to be a fresh expression of church; the latter more clearly is. What the gAp church attends to is that the process for faith generation among young people who do not have a church background still requires the mix of practices that link plausibility – meaning making – with generative experiences. The church is committed to working with and welcoming young people to any or all of the activities that it puts on, but linking these is vital for faith generation. In terms of Christian presence this has been reinforced through the new focus the church has, and is being extended as the work it is doing connects to wider roles in the community, such as the mentoring project.

Faith generation requires action to build intentional Christian communities within which young people can 'indwell and construct' faith identity. These 'places to be Christian' are unique in that they meet the needs of particular groups of young people. However, they will also have in common identifiable practices that help to affirm the plausibility of Christian belief, enable young people to explore identity and meaning, and engage in acts of faith that generate experience and engagement with God.

Conclusion

Faith generation – reversing discipleship decay and renewing the Church

In the Introduction I stressed that this would not be a 'how-to' but a 'why-how-to' book. The current experience of the Church is one where decline continues to be a threat. This decline is felt most acutely around the intergenerational transmission of faith. This reality is not going to go away and needs to be embraced as the 'new conditions' in which we are seeking to be church – to establish Christian presence.

Part of this reality is that faith in a secular age has particular characteristics, which if not directly addressed will continue to contribute towards decline – at the fault line of the transmission of faith between generations. These challenges revolve around the issues of *choice, sense* and *use*. Being Christian is a choice and a choice is made in relationship to scepticism and indifference. Making a choice to believe is one that has implications for a person's sense of identity, both positively and also in ways that open him or her up to conflict and challenge. Being Christian in such a secular age also means that we have to learn to detect and express how we sense God and to make sense of God in our lives. This sense of God comes through knowing as experience and by finding meaning in our experience of God. Being a person of faith connects us to a lifestyle that we draw on and fall back to. At times we will need to use the group of Christians around us for support and reassurance. At other times we might rely on prayer to help manage our questions and concerns. In time we might also find that we can be used by God to act in the world and connect with him in new ways. Faith is implausible to some, but impossible to let go of once you have discovered it.

The process of forming such a faith is not one that naturally occurs; we need to move from a mindset of faith development to one of faith generation. Faith formation for young people in a secular age is a process of indwelling and constructing, of building upon the faith they were raised in so as to understand it for themselves, or of adopting the faith they have been exposed to because it helps to make more sense of who they are. It is a process that requires us to connect with a community that understands this task and has experience of this. Youth ministry is vital to help create such places, places where faith becomes more plausible, more meaningful and more tangible.

Reversing the decline in the number of young people in the Church requires faith generation. Being intentional about this activity requires attention to how we form places and groups within which young people can find the plausibility, identity and reliability practices to shape faith for the secular age in which they live. Where churches are engaged in faith generation among children and young people, this activity spills over into the other areas where they are seeking to establish Christian presence. Where churches are bold and engage young people outside the Church, this presence is similarly extended.

Faith generation takes a different shape in different contexts. In each, though, it is focused on the same outcome: enabling young people to indwell and construct faith identity – a faith that is not only new for each generation, but also lasting. If we don't engage in faith generation then reversing this decline and extending this impact is unlikely. We will not grow as a Church in numbers or depth. This is why we need to take urgent action 'to focus on children, young people and their parents and a challenge to identify how the church can best invest in people, programmes and strategies which will encourage young people actively to continue exploring faith'.[1] We begin this by deciding to do so.

---

[1] *From Anecdote to Evidence: Findings from the Church Growth Research Programme 2011–13* (London: The Church of England, 2014), 24.

Bibliography

Aiken, Nick. *Working with Teenagers: The Essential Handbook.* New rev. edn. London: Marshall Pickering, 1994.

Anderson, E. B. 'A Constructive Task in Religious Education: Making Christian Selves.' *Religious Education* 93, no. 2 (1998): 173–88.

Arweck, Elisabeth, and James A. Beckford. 'Social Perspectives.' In *Religion and Change in Modern Britain,* edited by Linda Woodhead and Rebecca Catto, 352–72. London/New York: Routledge, 2012.

Astley, Jeff. *Ordinary Theology: Looking, Listening and Learning in Theology.* Explorations in Pastoral, Practical, and Empirical Theology. Aldershot: Ashgate, 2002.

Baigent, Avril. *The Y Church Report.* Northampton: Youth Office of the Roman Catholic Diocese, 2003.

Baker, Dori Grinenko. *Doing Girlfriend Theology: God-Talk with Young Women.* Cleveland, OH: Pilgrim Press, 2005.

Baker, Dori Grinenko. 'Evoking Testimony through Holy Listening: The Art of Interview as a Practice in Youth Ministry.' *Journal of Youth and Theology* 4, no. 2 (November 2005): 53–68.

Bass, Dorothy C. *Life Together: Practicing Faith with Adolescents.* Princeton Lectures on Youth Church and Culture, 2000. Edited by Princeton Theological Seminary Institute for Youth Ministry. Princeton, NJ: Princeton Theological Seminary, 2001.

Bass, Dorothy C. 'On the Bearing of a Living Tradition.' *Religious Education* 98, no. 4 (2003): 503–10.

Bass, Dorothy C., and Don C. Richter. *Way to Live: Christian Practices for Teens.* Nashville, TN: Upper Room Books, 2002.

Beckwith, Ivy. *Postmodern Children's Ministry: Ministry to Children in the 21st Century.* El Cajon, CA: Youth Specialties, 2004.

Borgman, Dean. *When Kumbaya Is Not Enough: A Practical Theology for Youth Ministry.* Peabody, MA: Hendrickson, 1997.

Brierley, Danny. *Growing Community: Making Groups Work with Young People.* Youthwork: The Resources (Developing Practice). Series edited by Danny Brierley and John Buckeridge. Carlisle/Waynesboro, GA: Authentic Lifestyle, 2003.

Brierley, Danny. *Joined Up: An Introduction to Youthwork and Ministry*. Youthwork: The Resources (Going Deeper). Series edited by Danny Brierley and John Buckeridge. Carlisle: Authentic Lifestyle, 2003.

Brierley, Peter. *Pulling Out of the Nosedive: A Contemporary Picture of Churchgoing: What the 2005 English Church Census Reveals*. London: Christian Research, 2006.

Brierley, Peter. *Reaching and Keeping Teenagers*. Tunbridge Wells/London: MARC/Christian Research, 1993.

Brierley, Peter. *Reaching and Keeping Tweenagers: Analysis of the 2001 Rakes Survey*. London: Christian Research, 2002.

Brierley, Peter. *The Tide Is Running Out*. London: Christian Research Association, 2001.

Church Growth Research Project Report on Strand 3b: An Analysis of Fresh Expressions of Church and Church Plants Begun in the Period 1992–2012. Sheffield: Church Army Research Unit, 2013.

Collins-Mayo, Sylvia, Bob Mayo, Sally Nash and Christopher Cocksworth. *The Faith of Generation Y*. Explorations. London: Church House Publishing, 2010.

Cray, Graham. *Youth Congregations and the Emerging Church*. Grove Evangelism Series. Cambridge: Grove, 2002.

Crockett, A., and D. Voas. 'Generations of Decline: Religious Change in 20th-Century Britain'. *Journal for the Scientific Study of Religion* 45, no. 4 (2006): 567–84.

Davie, Grace. *Europe: The Exceptional Case: Parameters of Faith in the Modern World*. Sarum Theological Lectures. London: Darton, Longman & Todd, 2002.

Day, David, and Philip May. *Teenage Beliefs*. Oxford: Lion, 1991.

Dean, Kenda Creasy. *Almost Christian: What the Faith of Our Teenagers Is Telling the American Church*. New York: Oxford University Press, 2010.

Dean, Kenda Creasy. *Practicing Passion: Youth and the Quest for a Passionate Church*. Grand Rapids, MI: Eerdmans, 2004.

Dean, Kenda Creasy. 'Theological Rocks – First Things First'. In *Starting Right: Thinking Theologically about Youth Ministry*, edited by Kenda Creasy Dean, Chap Clark and Dave Rahn, 15–39. Grand Rapids, MI: Zondervan, 2001.

Dean, Kenda Creasy, and Ron Foster. *The Godbearing Life: The Art of Soul Tending for Youth Ministry*. Nashville, TN: Upper Room Books, 1998.

Dearnley, Ruth. 'Church Hall vs Lychgate: Which Young People Should We Focus Our Mission Efforts On?' In *Young People + Mission: A Practical Guide*, edited by Alison Booker and David Booker, 133–45. London: Church House Publishing, 2007.

Devadason, R. 'Constructing Coherence? Young Adults' Pursuit of Meaning through Multiple Transitions between Work, Education and Unemployment.' *Journal of Youth Studies* 10, no. 2 (2007): 203–21.

DeVries, Mark. *Family-Based Youth Ministry: Reaching the Been-There, Done-That Generation.* Downer's Grove, IL: IVP, 1994.

Dykstra, Craig R., and Dorothy C. Bass. 'A Theological Understanding of Christian Practices.' In *Practicing Theology: Beliefs and Practices in Christian Life*, edited by Miroslav Volf and Dorothy C. Bass, 13–32. Grand Rapids, MI/Cambridge: Eerdmans, 2002.

Ellis, John W. 'Informal Education: A Christian Perspective.' In *Using Informal Education: An Alternative to Casework, Teaching and Control?*, edited by Tony Jeffs and Mark Smith, 89–100. Innovations in Education. Milton Keynes: Open University Press, 1990.

Ellis, John W. 'Youth Work and Evangelism – Can They Co-Exist with Integrity?' *Perspectives: Journal of Reflective Youth Work Practice and Applied Theology* (Summer 1998): 10–12.

Emery-Wright, Steve. *Passionate Worship: Hearing the Voices of Young People.* Monograph Series. Cambridge: YTC Press, 2009.

Farley, Edward. 'Can Church Education Be Theological Education?' In *Theological Perspectives on Christian Formation: A Reader on Theology and Christian Education*, edited by Jeff Astley, Leslie J. Francis and Colin Crowder, 31–44. Leominster: Gracewing, 1996.

Farley, Edward. *Theologia: The Fragmentation and Unity of Theological Education.* Philadelphia: Fortress Press, 1983.

Finney, John. *Finding Faith Today: How Does It Happen?* Swindon: British and Foreign Bible Society, 1992.

Fowler, James W. 'The Emerging New Shape of Practical Theology.' In *Practical Theology: International Perspectives*, edited by Friedrich Schweitzer and Johannes A. van der Ven, 75–92. Erfahrung und Theologie, Bd 340172-1135. Frankfurt am Main/New York: P. Lang, 1999.

Fowler, James W. 'Practical Theology and Theological Education: Some Models and Questions.' *Theology Today* 42, no. 1 (April 1985): 43–58.

From Anecdote to Evidence: Findings from the Church Growth Research Programme 2011–13. London: The Church of England, 2014.

Gardner, Jason. *Mend the Gap: Can the Church Reconnect the Generations?* Nottingham: IVP, 2008.

Graham, Elaine L. *Transforming Practice: Pastoral Theology in an Age of Uncertainty.* London: Mowbray, 1996.

Grapes, Christine. 'Developing Contextual Models of Youth Ministry, Part 1.' *Youth and Theology* 4, no. 1 (April 2005): 67–81.

Green, Maxine, and Chandu Christian. *Accompanying Young People on Their Spiritual Quest*. London: National Society/Church House Publishing, 1998.

Guest, Mathew. *Evangelical Identity and Contemporary Culture: A Congregational Study in Innovation*. Studies in Evangelical History and Thought. Milton Keynes: Paternoster Press, 2007.

Heelas, Paul, and Linda Woodhead. *The Spiritual Revolution: Why Religion Is Giving Way to Spirituality*. Religion in the Modern World. Malden, MA/Oxford: Blackwell, 2005.

Heywood, David. 'Theology or Social Science? The Theoretical Basis for Christian Education.' In *The Contours of Christian Education*, edited by Jeff Astley and David Day, Chapter 7. Great Wakering: McCrimmons, 1992.

Immink, Gerrit. *Faith: A Practical Theological Reconstruction*. Studies in Practical Theology. Grand Rapids, MI/Cambridge: Eerdmans, 2005.

Jackson, Bob. *What Makes Churches Grow? Vision and Practice in Effective Mission*. London: Church House Publishing, 2015.

Kay, William K., and Leslie J. Francis. *Drift from the Churches: Attitude toward Christianity during Childhood and Adolescence*. Religion, Culture and Society. Cardiff: University of Wales Press, 1996.

Kinnaman, David, and Aly Hawkins. *You Lost Me: Why Young Christians Are Leaving Church – and Rethinking Faith*. Grand Rapids, MI: Baker, 2011.

Loukes, Harold. *Teenage Religion: An Enquiry into Attitudes and Possibilities among British Boys and Girls in Secondary Modern Schools*. London: SCM Press, 1961. Published on behalf of the Institute of Christian Education.

MacLaren, Duncan. *Mission Implausible: Restoring Credibility to the Church*. Studies in Religion and Culture. Milton Keynes: Paternoster Press, 2004.

Madge, Nicola, Peter J. Hemming, Kevin Stenson and Nick Allum. *Youth on Religion: The Development, Negotiation and Impact of Faith and Non-Faith Identity*. Hove/New York: Routledge, 2014.

Miles, Steven. *Youth Lifestyles in a Changing World*. Buckingham/Philadelphia: Open University Press, 2000.

Morisy, Ann. *Journeying Out: A New Approach to Christian Mission*. London/New York: Morehouse, 2004.

Nash, Sally, Sylvia Collins-Mayo and Bob Mayo. 'Raising Christian Consciousness: Creating Place.' *Journal of Youth and Theology* 6, no. 2 (2007): 41–59.

Nash, Sally, and Jo Whitehead, eds. *Christian Youth Work in Theory and Practice: A Handbook*. London: SCM Press, 2014.

Nel, Malan. 'Identity Formation and the Challenge of Individuation in Youth Ministry.' *Journal of Youth Ministry* 1, no. 2 (Spring 2003): 79–102.

Nel, Malan. *Youth Ministry: An Inclusive Congregational Approach.* Brooklyn/ Pretoria: Malan Nel, 2000.

Passmore, Richard. *Off the Beaten Track: A Fresh Approach to Youth Work and Church Based on Jesus' Travels.* Edited by Jenny Baker. Birmingham: Christian Education, 2004.

Passmore, Richard, Lorimer J. Passmore and James G. Ballantyne. *Here Be Dragons: Youth Work and Mission Off the Map.* Birmingham: Porthouse, 2013.

Passmore, Richard, Jo Pimlott and Nigel Pimlott. *Meet Them Where They're At: Helping Churches Engage Young People through Detached Youth Work.* Bletchley: Scripture Union, 2003.

Peterson, Eugene H. *Like Dew Your Youth: Growing Up with Your Teenager.* Grand Rapids, MI: Eerdmans, 1994.

Rankin, Phil. *Buried Spirituality: A Report on the Findings of the Fellowship in the Spirituality of Young People Based at Sarum College, Salisbury.* Salisbury: Sarum College Press, 2005.

Richter, Don C., Doug Magnuson and Michael Baizerman. 'Re-Conceiving Youth Ministry.' *Religious Education* 93, no. 3 (1998): 339–57.

Riley, Naomi Schaefer. *Got Religion? How Churches, Mosques, and Synagogues Can Bring Young People Back.* West Conshohocken, PA: Templeton Press, 2014.

Roeland, Johan. *Selfation: Dutch Evangelical Youth between Subjectivization and Subjection.* Amsterdam: Pallas Proefschriften/Amsterdam University Press, 2009.

Root, Andrew. *Revisiting Relational Youth Ministry: From Strategy of Influence to a Theology of Incarnation.* Downer's Grove, IL: IVP, 2007.

Root, Andrew, and Kenda Creasy Dean. *The Theological Turn in Youth Ministry.* Downer's Grove, IL: IVP, 2011.

Russell, Chris. 'A Church for the Unchurched.' In *Church Unlimited: Youthwork and Mission Today,* edited by Nicholas Shepherd and Jonathan Brant, 33–43. Leicester: Youthwork the Partnership/Matador, 2008.

Savage, Sara B., Sylvia Collins-Mayo and Bob Mayo with Graham Cray. *Making Sense of Generation Y: The World View of 15- to 25-Year-Olds.* Explorations. London: Church House Publishing, 2006.

Schweitzer, Friedrich. *The Postmodern Life Cycle: Challenges for Church and Theology.* St Louis, MO: Chalice Press, 2004.

Senter, Mark H. 'The Three-Legged Stool of Youth Ministry.' In *Agenda for Youth Ministry: Cultural Themes in Faith and Church,* edited by Dean Borgman and Christine Cook, 24–35. London: SPCK, 1998.

Senter, Mark H., Wesley Black, Chap Clark and Malan Nel. *Four Views of Youth Ministry and the Church: Inclusive Congregational, Preparatory, Missional, Strategic.* Grand Rapids, MI: Zondervan, 2001.

Bibliography

Smith, Christian, and Melinda Lundquist Denton. *Soul Searching: The Religious and Spiritual Lives of American Teenagers*. Oxford/New York: Oxford University Press, 2005.

Smith, James K. A. *How (Not) to Be Secular: Reading Charles Taylor*. Grand Rapids, MI: Eerdmans, 2014.

Swinton, John, and Harriet Mowat. *Practical Theology and Qualitative Research*. London: SCM Press, 2005.

Tanner, Kathryn. 'Theological Reflection and Christian Practices.' In *Practicing Theology: Beliefs and Practices in Christian Life*, edited by Miroslav Volf and Dorothy C. Bass, 228–42. Grand Rapids, MI/Cambridge: Eerdmans, 2002.

Tanner, Kathryn. *Theories of Culture: A New Agenda for Theology*. Guides to Theological Inquiry. Minneapolis, MN: Fortress Press, 1997.

Taylor, Charles. *A Secular Age*. Cambridge, MA/London: Belknap, 2007.

Voas, David. 'Children and Youth Ministry and Church Growth.' *Praxeis* 1, no. 1 (2014): 3–8.

Voas, David, and Alasdair Crockett. 'Religion in Britain: Neither Believing nor Belonging.' *Sociology* 39, no. 1 (1 February 2005): 11–28.

Ward, Pete. 'Christian Relational Care.' In *Relational Youthwork*, edited by Pete Ward, 13–40. Oxford/Sutherland, Australia: Lynx/Albatross Books, 1995.

Ward, Pete. 'Distance and Closeness: Finding the Right Ecclesial Context for Youth Ministry.' In *The Church and Youth Ministry*, edited by Pete Ward, 34–49. Oxford: Lynx, 1995.

Ward, Pete. *Growing up Evangelical: Youthwork and the Making of a Subculture*. London: SPCK, 1996.

Ward, Pete. *Participation and Mediation: A Practical Theology for the Liquid Church*. London: SCM Press, 2008.

Ward, Pete. *Youth Culture and the Gospel*. London: Marshall Pickering, 1992.

Ward, Pete. *Youthwork and the Mission of God*. Frameworks for Relational Outreach. London: SPCK, 1997.

Ward, Pete, and Lindsay Urwin, eds. *Youthful Spirit*. London: Tufton Books/The Church Union, 1998.

Warren, Michael. *Youth Gospel Liberation*. 3rd edn. Dublin: Veritas, 1998. 1987.

Wellings, Martin, and Andrew Wood. 'Facets of Formation: Theology through Training.' In *Unmasking Methodist Theology*, edited by Clive Marsh, 70–83. New York/London: Continuum, 2004.

Westerhoff, John H. 'A Call to Catechesis.' *The Living Light* 14, no. 3 (1977), 354–8.

Westerhoff, John H. *Will Our Children Have Faith?* Rev. edn. Harrisburg, PA: Morehouse, 2000. 1976.

Westerhoff, John H., and Gwen Kennedy Neville. *Generation to Generation: Conversations on Religious Education and Culture.* 2nd edn. New York: Pilgrim Press, 1979.

White, David F. *Practicing Discernment with Youth: A Transformative Youth Ministry Approach.* Youth Ministry Alternatives. Cleveland, OH: Pilgrim Press, 2005.

Yaconelli, Mark. *Contemplative Youth Ministry.* London: SPCK, 2006.

Young, Kerry. *The Art of Youth Work.* 2nd edn. Lyme Regis: Russell House, 2006. 1996.

Did you know that SPCK is a registered charity?

As well as publishing great books by leading Christian authors, we also . . .

. . . **make assemblies meaningful and fun for over a million children** by running www.assemblies.org.uk, a popular website that provides free assembly scripts for teachers. For many children, school assembly is the only contact they have with Christian faith and culture, and the only time in their week for spiritual reflection.

. . . **help prisoners to become confident readers** with our easy-to-read stories. Poor literacy is a huge barrier to rehabilitation. Prisoners identify with the believable heroes of our gritty fiction. At the same time, questions at the end of each chapter help them to examine their choices from a moral perspective and to build their reading confidence.

. . . **support student ministers overseas in their training** through partnerships in the Global South.

Please support these great schemes: visit www.spck.org.uk/support-us to find out more.